This book is dedicated to all Peace Corps volunteers who have served and will serve in Cameroon.

Acknowledgements

Very special thanks to my sister, Darleen Guien, for sharing this trip, giving valuable insights, providing photos and excerpts from her travel log, editing, and proofreading

Thanks also to Michael Breyer, George Gati, and Donald Leach for additional editing and proof reading

Paul J. Hamel
2851 Amatista Court
Palm Springs, CA 92264
Cell Phone: 310-991-2374
Email: paulhamel@twc.com

The Cover

The mandala represents different symbols of Cameroon.

TABLE OF CONTENTS

INTRODUCTION

I was a Peace Corps volunteer in Cameroon from 1969 to 1972. I've always wanted to go back to Bafia, the town I lived in, to see how it has changed over the last four decades. Because of my professional responsibilities as a school administrator, the cost of the trip, the extensive planning that would be required, and not wanting to travel alone, I never got around to it. Also, I didn't want to travel with my spouse because I was very concerned about how a gay married couple would be treated, and I didn't want to find out. Cameroon is not known for being a gay-friendly place.

Paul and Darleen take a "selfie" photo on the Lobe River

One day in January 2013, my sister, Darleen Guien, who lived with me in Cameroon in 1971 and who married my French roommate at the time, made a suggestion that we both go back to Cameroon together before we get any older. She was in Ecuador for two months visiting friends and said that visiting a third world country was difficult, but doable. She suggested that we plan on taking the trip as soon as we could. It was important for us to go back together considering the wealth of memories and experiences we had had there. The time was right; we were both retired and had enough money from a project we had both worked on together to pay for our trip. We are good travel partners and have traveled together many times before. I knew that I would feel comfortable with her because we both spoke French and were familiar with the culture. Also, I assumed that most people would treat us as a couple, which in fact, they did.

It didn't take me long to think about Darleen's proposal; I jumped at the opportunity, so we began planning. We settled on staying fifteen days with a two-day layover in Paris where I could get used to the time difference and do some last minute shopping. Darleen was already in France, where she had lived for 30 years, and arranged for me to stay where she was staying at a friend's home just outside of Paris.

We couldn't visit all of Cameroon so we decided to visit only parts of the country we already

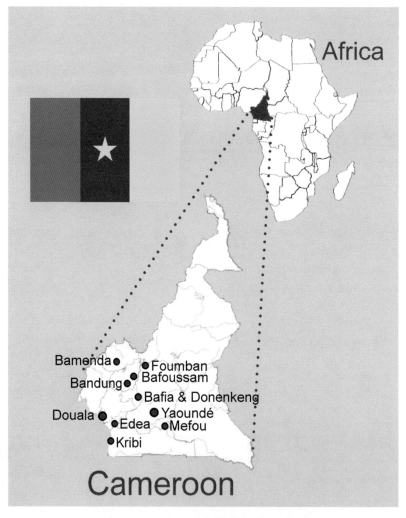

Africa

Bamenda
Foumban
Bandung
Bafoussam
Bafia & Donenkeng
Douala
Yaoundé
Edea
Mefou
Kribi

Cameroon

knew. Our itinerary included Yaoundé, Bafia, Kribi, and Bafoussam, from which we would take day trips to Bamenda and Foumban. These cities are located in the center, east, and south of the country. We opted not to visit areas near the Nigerian border or in the extreme north where we were concerned for our safety.

Dollies Making A Difference is an organization of women who sew cloth dollies and colorful teddy bears with love and compassion for children all over the world.

For more information, please visit our website:
www.dolliesmakingadifference.com

We chose to go during the month of September even though it was the rainy season, because we wanted to be there during the school year. We hoped that the rainy season would provide some relief from the extreme heat of the dry season. In the rainy season it rains almost every day; however, only for short periods at a time, usually at dusk. Also, thanks to paved roads, we hoped that travelling between cities would be much easier now than years ago

APE ACTION AFRICA
Mefou Primate Sanctuary, Cameroon
www.apeactionafrica.org/index

when we had to travel on dirt roads that often turned into impassable mud holes and ruts.

We didn't want to be just tourists, so we decided to do something active, exciting and meaningful, keeping with the old Peace Corps spirit. Darleen volunteered to become an ambassador for *Dollies Making a Difference*, an organization of women who make dolls and teddy bears, and another group of women in Santa Barbara who make dresses for needy children called *Little Dresses for Africa*. Darleen was able to collect 50 pounds of toys and dresses that neatly fit into a large piece of luggage—one of the two that I was allowed to take. Her plan was to find an orphanage or pre-school in our former town, Bafia,

This photo was taken by Elvis, our guide.

and distribute them to needy children. Although we were not able to find an orphanage, we did find two pre-schools where the dolls, teddy bears, dresses, bags of individually wrapped pieces of hard candy, toothbrushes, and school supplies were distributed.

As for myself, I chose to organize a fund-raiser at home for the Mefou Primate Sanctuary where orphan chimps and gorillas are cared for. Primates have a special place in my heart since I cared for a baby baboon while serving in Bafia. I also babysat a baby chimp for a short

Paul with Julette, a baby baboon in 1971

time. I managed to raise $1,000 from my friends and planned on presenting the money in cash to the director of the sanctuary during my visit there. Before our visit I contacted the director of the program in England and was told that giving cash directly to the on-site director at the sanctuary would be the best way to donate. Bringing that much cash is risky, but I did it anyway. It turned out to be one of the highlights of my trip.

I also brought several 8"x10" glossy photos in cardboard certificate holders to give as presents. Two rare photos were for the Préfet of Bafia: one of the Prefecture building

3

in 1969 and the other of a parade celebrating the 10th anniversary of Cameroon's independence, held in front of the Prefecture in 1970. The Préfet seemed very surprised and pleased with these unexpected gifts. He promised to display the photos in his office.

Another photo was of the house I lived in during my stay in Bafia. I had planned on giving it to whoever lived in the house at the present. It turned out that my former landlord still lived in the house so I gave it to him. He was extremely grateful. Another photo was of the house that Dr. and Mrs. Sandilands lived in while serving in Donenkeng, a village not far from Bafia in the 1960-70s. Again, I had planned to give it to the current tenants, but when I found the house, it was empty and abandoned. I ended up giving the photo to the pastor of the Presbyterian mission hospital. The last photo was of the school building I helped build on the mission site at the Anderson School in 1971. The school building was no longer in use; it has no roof and the walls were barely visible due to overgrown vines and tall grass. It broke my heart to see it. However, newer buildings make up the school, which is now a government-run lyceé. I can't be too sad because it did last for many years. I gave the photo to the director of the lyceé.

I also brought an unconventional gift: several hundred condoms that were donated by WeHo Life, a program funded by the City of West Hollywood. Before the trip,

I had no idea how I would distribute them so I decided to "play it by ear" and see what would happen when I got there. It turned out that my former landlord's niece, Chantal, who was in Bafia for the funeral of her mother, was an AIDS activist. I noticed that she was wearing an AIDS (SIDA in French) pin and carried a purse with a logo from an AIDS organization. When I told her that I had brought condoms, she immediately volunteered to take them to a local clinic. Since then, she and I have stayed in contact.

A major personal goal of this trip was to write this book about my experiences in Cameroon. I finished the first part, *My Life in Bafia*, and I wanted to write a second part, *Return to Cameroon*, which would be about how the country had changed over the years. I also wanted the book to provide some general information as well as some insights into Cameroonian life that may be useful for travelers who plan on visiting Cameroon in the future.

Another goal was to visit the main post office in Yaoundé to buy stamps for my collection. I have collected stamps all my life and have one of the most extensive collections of Cameroonian stamps in the world. I was fortunate to find the main philatelic office and bought many current stamps to fill in the gaps in my collection.

4

PREPARING
FOR OUR TRIP

Who said that getting ready for a trip is half the fun? Not in this case. Preparing for our trip took us a lot of time and thought, especially since we were traveling on our own. Cameroon is not a well-known tourist destination, and seeing tourists there is not common. The only "real" tourist area that attracts Europeans is Kribi, which is located in the southwest corner of the country. We didn't think of our trip to Cameroon as a vacation but rather an adventure, knowing that there might be some "challenges" during our stay. Looking back at our planning, we did pretty well anticipating what we would need. For those of you who plan on your own adventure, here are a few tips.

GROUND TRANSPORTATION

The only real concern we had in planning our trip was ground transportation. We didn't want to take crowded buses and taxis. We had done that forty years ago, and we were not ready to do it again, especially at our age. So, we took the chance and arrived not knowing how we would manage to get around. We were relying on our hotels to identify drivers for us. We were right. Our hotels managed to find us drivers for a day and for long trips as well. The cars were not luxurious, but they were adequate for our needs. A benefit of having a professional driver is that he can also serve as a local guide as well as a bodyguard. Hiring a driver may seem expensive, but it is not in comparison to personal drivers in the U.S., and it is well worth the cost. During our trip, we paid an average of 30,000 CFA ($15) for day trips in and around Yaoundé, Bafoussam, and Kribi. During our longer distant trips, we paid an average of 70,000 CFA ($35) per day. For long trips, the price of gas, tolls, and the cost of driver's food and lodging are extra. On average, long trips cost us about $60 per day.

Below: Dieu-Donné, our driver, and Darleen overlooking Yaounde from Mount Fébé

Motorcycles also serve as taxis.

6

A typical bus and taxi in Yaounde

GETTING AROUND THE COUNTRY

Getting a Taxi from the Nsimalen International Airport to Yaoundé

The hotel hadn't sent anyone to pick us up. So we asked the policeman again about getting a taxi. He took us out to the parking area (leaving his security post!) and shooing away a few drivers that he called thieves, he found us a driver, who was a cousin, for sure. ... We got into the rather dilapidated taxi hoping we would get out alive after the 27-km ride from the airport to the city. We found the hotel, in a rather noisy and run-down neighborhood. We paid the driver who had actually been relatively safe and even good at explaining the layout of the city.

Taking Taxis or Hiring a Driver?

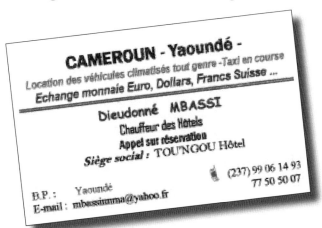

We inquired about the taxis at the front desk (of the Tou'Ngou Hotel) and they told us that it could be dangerous to get into just any taxi—especially the ones carrying other passengers. I remembered sharing taxis forty years ago without hesitation, but it had become difficult. They happened to have a taxi for the hotel. He would be a little more expensive but we would be safe. We were introduced to Dieudonné Mbassi, got into a rather beat up unmarked taxi and asked our driver to take us to the cathedral. ... He (turnedout to be) ... a safe, personable driver we could count on.

Yaoundé Traffic

Driving around the crowded streets was unnerving—too many taxis, people, stands lining the streets and spilling out into the traffic, no stop signs or lights, no obvious traffic rules. Dieudonné (our driver) just pushed his way through with the car, avoiding obstacles, verified that the doors were locked when there were a lot of people in the streets, made us keep the windows up in spite of the heat, and kept repeating that we had to be prudent.

A typical taxi

The Road to the Mefou Ape Sanctuary

We drove to the Ape Sanctuary about 45 minutes away. We passed through all kinds of neighborhoods—mostly poor and bustling. It still amazed me the amount of commerce going on. No one had much money but there was a lot of buying and selling, wheeling and dealing: "système D (or resourcefulness) par excellence". The neighborhood where the tank trucks filled up was interesting: jam packed with people, buses, vendors on the side of the road, huge trucks and the ubiquitous 5000 yellow taxis. Dieudonné (our driver) told us that a few years back a tanker truck exploded and many people died. This dangerous industrial zone slowly gave way to rural areas—clumps of houses, dilapidated schools, fields, meandering brick-red roads full of ruts, gullies, potholes more like craters, bordered by dense jungle vegetation. We could see the rain forest and its canopy of trees. And we were only a relatively distance from the capital city. *(Read more about the Mefou Ape Sanctuary on page 69.)*

The Mefou Ape Sanctuary

Getting a Traffic Ticket on the Way to Bafia

We stopped to pay the 500 CFA toll fee, which seemed to explain the road improvements. We passed glorious rain forest—so lush and green—canopy trees, banana palms, and cocoa nurseries. When we had passed Bokito there was a roadblock for safety checks (Sécurité Routière). Paul and I didn't have seat belts on. I hadn't even noticed them in this old, battered car where they were stuck under the seats. We got a fine of 1000 CFA for that plus the police officer suggested that we add 5000 CFA so the driver wouldn't get a ticket. He could have asked for a lot more, we didn't have much choice. By this time we were in the savannah—sparser trees, grasses and still stunningly beautiful. There were small villages along the way, huts made of mud and branches, lots of women carrying babies on their backs, children in uniform walking home from school. *(Read more about the trip on page 88.)*

Hiring a Driver in Bafoussam

Before even going to breakfast we asked the director of the Tatotel Hotel to get us a driver. The car would be a RAV4 and the driver would cost 60,000 CFA plus the price of gas. He didn't arrive until 10:30, a good hour later than expected. He filled up the tank which was a big mistake. It cost us 30,000 CFA (about $60, more than I pay in expensive Los Angeles). The trip we wanted only took about ¼ of a tank. I hated being taken for a piggy bank. He should have been more honest on that one.

Bafoussam Traffic

(We took) a quick trip to the supermarket a few doors down (from the Talotel Hotel) for picnic things (for our trip to Kribi). If the supermarket had been across the street I would have never gone. Crossing a street where the traffic was intense, where there were no obvious traffic rules, where cars even drove on the sidewalks, would have been suicidal. The few pedestrians trying to get to the other side of the road were literally risking their lives.

The Road to Bamenda from Bafoussam

The road was horrific: full of pot holes, speed bumps, tolls, trucks, mammy wagons, motorcycles, people passing on curves or speed bumps whether they could see or not—and especially, it seemed, if they could not see. We came to a few close calls. Our driver was a little too daring. As Paul said, "this is not for the faint of heart." On a few occasions we were even three abreast—cars passing cars that were already passing cars. It was reminiscent of the Pan American highway in Ecuador.

After two hours of bouncing in the back seat we arrived in Bamenda. The scenery on the way was beautiful: mountains, pine trees, eucalyptus trees, fields of corn, vegetables. This was obviously a rich agricultural area. We passed a few towns with farmer's markets teeming with people, tarps on the ground piled high with produce. There were also lots of people walking back from church, all in their Sunday best—Catholics, Jehovah's Witnesses, Presbyterians.

The Trip from Bafoussam to Kribi (via Douala and Edea)

So off we went. And it was the most harrowing trip I have ever taken in my life—and I have had some dillies. The driver hit the road at top speed as if possessed. We tried numerous times to get him to slow down, which he would do for a few minutes, then back to the fast and furious pace. He passed cars on curves with no visibility at all; he drove at breakneck speed down narrow roads where children were walking to school on both sides of the road. There were mothers and tiny kids that he sped by. Three year olds. And he expected them to move aside. I was going spare with anxiety. When we got to Douala it was horrifying—huge potholes in the streets, trucks, taxis, motorcycles coming from every direction. It was total chaos and there were no paved roads in the most industrial and commercial city in the country. The traffic was intense and trucks spewed polluting, black fumes. I suppose "smog tests"

don't exist. Our driver finally forced his way through this and took the wrong road to Edea, the next town on our trip. He went on the old, unpaved, pothole-littered road rather than the new one. We kept asking him to turn around because this could not possibly be the right road but he refused to listen. So we bounced and swerved every inch of the way. It was like a slalom navigating around the potholes and even driving through them too fast, when what had to happen, happened. He hit a crater of a pothole at breakneck speed, we heard an explosion, and we had a flat tire. The tire had been literally cut. So we stood by the side of this dirt road (careful to avoid areas with ants) and watched the driver change the tire. We stood there with our arms crossed, refusing to help in any way. He said he was a mechanic and changing the tire was no problem—even while wearing his beautiful white shoes. But I was a bit surprised that as a mechanic, he didn't respect the car more.

Flat tire on the way to Kribi

Finally after going through desolate jungle and tiny forlorn villages we arrived in Edea and could pick up the main road that we never should have left. The road was better but the driver was still irresponsible. It was a good thing that the Bishop of Bafia had asked God to protect us. Our guardian angels were probably exhausted by this point! *(Read more about this trip on page 146.)*

Our Driver in Kribi

We arranged for our taxi for the next day's trip to Yaoundé and for the day here in Kribi. The driver was recommended by the hotel and we crossed our fingers that he would be safer than the last one. His rates: 70,000 CFA for the trip to Yaoundé and 10,000 CFA in this tiny town. He took us to the Lobé Falls, which drop directly into the ocean. We took a boat ride up the river in a (barely) modern version of the pirogue.

Our driver Edie was a great tour guide. He pointed out things of interest, talked about the economy, global warming, life in Cameroon. He was an intelligent man, curious about everything. His formal education had been shortened and he only studied long enough to get a technical certificate (CAP) given after the 7th grade. He was the eldest and he had to go to work to support his family, working in a restaurant, driving a taxi, doing accounting services. One of his brothers was going to the university which must have made him very proud and bitter at the same time. But he said that that was the custom in Cameroon: the eldest was often sacrificed. But he was very smart and articulate with an excellent sense of customer service. He knew the importance of a good reputation in one's business. He had taken good care of a few doctors in the Doctors Without Borders/Médecins Sans Frontières and now he had a veritable roster. He seemed honest and hard-working and enterprising. We wish him nothing but the best.

The road (to the Lobé River and Falls) was to be widened to accommodate the trucks that would come from the new deepwater port. Many houses all along had a cross and A.D. written on them (à démolir, to be demolished). The resort hotels were right on the road. Our bungalow was a little bit off the road on a slight hill, but the restaurant was on a sliver of land between the road and the beach. It was slated for destruction and it had just been built. I fear that the noise and truck traffic in the future would ruin this little corner of paradise. It is called progress. But the people who profit from this will not be the average Cameroonian. For the moment the port is being built with mainly Chinese workers. At first, according to our driver, the project was 100% Chinese until the Cameroonians complained that there was no local job creation, so now about 20% are Cameroonian workers. The pipeline that will transport oil from Chad will end here, exports of wood and iron ore will follow; so much potential wealth that will inevitably fall into very few hands. The 1% indeed! The trip (from Kribi to Yaounde) was safe and uneventful, this driver was careful. We paid him the amount agreed upon and gave him a nice tip. He was visibly surprised and said that we spoiled him too much. *(Read more about this trip on page 162.)*

A Trip to Nsimalen International Airport from Yaoundé

The traffic that evening was absolutely horrible. No lights, no stop signs, a regular free for all. And it was Saturday night. It took forever just to advance a few yards. Luckily we had left well in advance. Once we had edged our way out of the city (praising Dieudonné's [our driver's] navigational skills) we still had 27 km to get to the airport. That part was easy. We parked and a young man in a green uniform came up with a trolley, loaded it and tackled the crowds in the terminal. We had no small change left so the porter got a 1000 CFA tip. He was ecstatic. We paid our driver in euros because we needed 20,000 CFA to get the exit stamp. You have to pay to get a visa to enter and pay to leave. We waved goodbye to our driver and started the marathon airport procedures. There were long lines to drop off the luggage, computers not cooperating at all, so lots of waiting. My case weighed in at 11 kg (instead of my usual 23) because there had been so little to buy. Once the suitcases were checked we had to pay the exit tax in a little office hidden behind the ticket counter. First passport check at the bottom of the stairs to go to the departure gates. Second passport check at the top of the stairs. Third check at passport control. Fourth check to get into the security area. Fifth check inside the security area. Then all carry on bags were x-rayed and thoroughly searched and any water bottles thrown away. Sixth passport check as you exited the security area, then a second check of luggage. Seventh passport check to go to the seating area. It was so completely absurd and inefficient. Nobody trusted anybody to do the job properly. We sat down in the waiting area—no food, no water, only two toilets. We had 5000 CFA left and had hoped to spend it on our last Cameroonian beers. No beer to buy! We got on the plane on time and it was, once again, totally packed. Every seat taken and lots of carry-on bags that didn't fit into the bins. The flight attendants came through the cabin with some kind of insecticide and sprayed everyone and everything, all the while reassuring us that it was completely non-toxic. We took off at 11:30 p.m., had a horrible meal that wasn't even edible, slept fitfully and after a six hour flight we arrived in Paris. I could have kissed the ground!

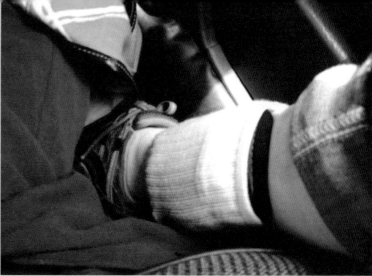

SAFETY

We were always aware of our surroundings. Bringing and wearing expensive jewelry is not recommended and can make you a target, so we didn't bring any. Although I felt completely safe during our trip, there is always a chance of something going wrong. It's best to have a local with you, especially if you are not travelling in a group. Having a private driver increases the chances of everything going smoothly because drivers also serve as additional security. When traveling by car, we didn't put the windows all the way down when going through crowded areas. Our drivers always made sure that the car doors were locked. Prevention is a key element to staying safe. We avoided taking taxis in Yaoundé because there is a risk of being robbed. Although taxis are inexpensive and plentiful, to get from one place to another, especially when there are other passengers in the car, can be very uncomfortable and take a long time. We knew not to go out at night, not only for our personal safety, but also because it gets dark quickly and there are no or few street lights. During a new moon, it is pitch black outside, and people can't see even an inch in front of their noses. There is total darkness. On the other hand, during a full moon, a newspaper can easily be read outside!

TAKING PHOTOS

We had no problems taking photos. We tried to be as discreet as possible. In fact, Darleen and I took around 3000 still photos and 40 short videos. We used our iPhones and a small Minolta camera. I used these photos for the second half of this e-book. I also wanted to post some of the photos of Bafia on Google Earth. Before taking photos in Bafia, I asked the Préfet if it was okay to go around town and take photos of government buildings. He gave me his blessing, and he was pleased that Bafia would be put "on the map," literally. Check out the photos on Google Earth.

LANGUAGE

French is the dominant language, which almost everyone speaks in addition to their own native language. Almost everyone speaks some English since Cameroon is officially a bilingual country and English is taught in every school. Although West Cameroon is an English-speaking area of the country, everyone I encountered there spoke French fairly well. On the other hand, everyone I met in the French-speaking part of the country spoke only halting English.

Knowing French greatly enhanced our trip and allowed us to communicate with everyone we came in contact with. We spoke French most of the time. We were fortunate to have come from a French-speaking family, and we had lived in Cameroon for a few years, so we were familiar with the culture, their particular accent, vocabulary, and expressions. On occasion we did speak some English; however, it was for short periods of time, mostly when someone wanted to practice their English with us. We also heard West African Pidgin English, which is widely spoken, especially in the western part of the country. It is a language that developed as a trading language that sounds very similar to Standard English.

LUGGAGE

Most flights to Cameroon allow for two large pieces of luggage. (Check with the airline.) Theft is common so it is best to carry important documents, money, medication, and jewelry on your person or in a carry-on bag. To prevent theft many travelers have whole pieces of luggage wrapped in clear plastic cellophane at the airport in Europe. At first I didn't realize that wrapping luggage in cellophane was for security. In my case when the luggage arrived at the collection area, we made sure that we kept our luggage near us at all times because there were so many people scrambling around. We tried to find a luggage cart, but there were not enough for everyone. Porters guarded the remaining ones and didn't let them go until they were hired.

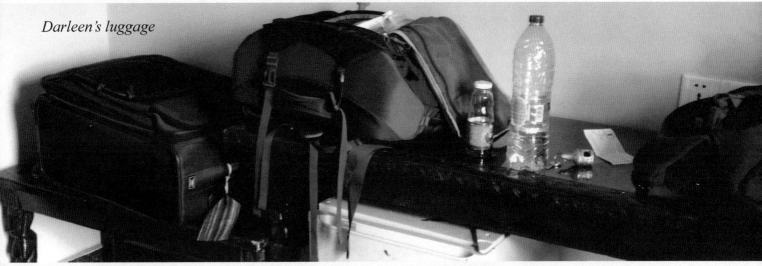

Darleen's luggage

TELEPHONES

Having a cell phone is absolutely necessary! We decided not to use our phones in Cameroon because there was no plan available. Instead, we bought an expensive Nokia cell phone one for around $20. It was the first thing we did when we got there. We had our driver call one of his contacts. He drove us to a place near Kennedy Boulevard and we bought a phone without leaving the car. One problem I had was forgetting to turn off my data roaming. This resulted in a $300 bill which was later reduced to $30. To charge our phones we used a regular European converter plug. When we left the country, we gave the phone to our driver as a gift. We used our iPhones only to take photos and check our e-mail wherever there was access to Wi-Fi.

HEALTH

Malaria is still a threat, so we made sure to take anti-malarial medicine that we got from our doctor. We also brought an anti-malarial device that emits a mist when it's plugged into an electrical outlet, a tube of sunscreen, and a tube of Benadryl triple antibiotic ointment for scratches and insect bites. Bugs are everywhere, especially cockroaches and ants. They are more of a nuisance than a real threat. I took along a spray bottle and packets of "OFF" which were very useful. At night I sprayed the legs of my bed with OFF to keep bugs--especially spiders--away. During our trip, Darleen got spider bites in several places on her arm during our stay in Kribi. They weren't serious bites, but just enough to cause discomfort and itching. In case of severe diarrhea, we took along a lot of Imodium and Cipro, for which we got prescriptions from our doctors. I took Cipro once and it made me sicker. Dehydration is a big and real problem. To prevent it, we made a point to always have bottled water with us. Once I got dehydrated to the point of getting muscle cramps. From that time onward, I forced myself to drink water, even if I wasn't thirsty.

HOTELS

Before arriving in Cameroon, we contacted and made reservations at four hotels by phoning directly and by email. Although we wanted to stay at the Hilton in Yaoundé, it was excessively expensive, so we decided to stay at the Hotel Tou'Ngou (B.P 3626 Carrefour Etoa - Meki, Yaoundé, 003626 Cameroon|1-866-925-9750). It was recommended by Peace Corps volunteers. We paid $56 per night—a much better rate than $250+ rate at the Hilton. More expensive rooms were also available at our hotel, but we decided on the least expensive ones because we didn't plan on spending much time in our rooms except for sleeping. The rooms were clean, had a bathroom with hot and cold water, TV, and air conditioning. The only major challenge was the loud music late at night.

In Bafia we stayed at the Hotel Rim Touristique (Rim A Ngam, Directeur-General) Center of town (237) 22 28 50 53 / (237) 99 53 96 99. It is the only "real" hotel in Bafia. It cost us about $20 per day. We splurged by staying at the Hotel Talotel, in Bafoussam; we spent $100 per room for three nights—the most we paid during our trip. It is considered the best hotel in the area with king size beds, a large modern bathroom, small refrigerator, air conditioning, TV, room service, and a swimming pool. The hotel also has an indoor and outdoor restaurant, bar, and night club.

In Kribi we stayed at the Hotel Les Gites, where we rented a bungalow in a resort setting overlooking the ocean. It contained two bedrooms and two bathrooms, a full kitchen, and a living room with air conditioning and a flat screen television. We spent about $40 per night—the going rate for the slow season. Many of the other hotels in Kribi were closed until the beginning of the dry season when visitors from the north flock to this beautiful seaside retreat.

Hotel Rim Touristique in Bafia

HOTEL REVIEWS

Tou'Ngou Hotel, Yaoundé

Carrefour Etoa-Meki, B.P. 3626 Yaounde.
(237) 22 20 10 25 Fax: 22 20 10 26
www. toungouhotel.com • E-mail: info@toungouhotel.com

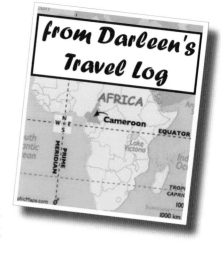

from Darleen's Travel Log

We found the hotel, in a rather noisy and run-down neighborhood. We paid the driver who had actually been relatively safe and even good at explaining the layout of the city. Our rooms were on the top floor in the old part of the hotel, up many, many flights of stairs and down long corridors. Two men brought up our bags. They each put the heaviest suitcase on their heads and carried the second bag. I could barely lift the bag onto a table, let alone onto my head. I opened the door to my room—a real dive. Walls in need of painting, fluorescent lights, doubtful bedding, and a bathroom shower that was just a hole in the floor with a shower hose. I killed a cockroach as soon as I crossed the threshold. Welcome to Africa! The room was not that expensive, but it was still about $50 a night. I was just hoping the bed was decent, which it was.

The lobby of the Tou'Ngou Hotel

Before bed we decided to go up to the terrace bar and have a celebratory beer. It was actually nice with a beautiful view of the city lights and a singer at the piano. We were very content with a few cold beers and some roasted peanuts.

Once in bed the noise from a nearby nightclub was deafening. It was as if the club patrons were dancing in my room. I was expecting it to stop at 2 a.m., but no, the last techno beat stopped at 5 a.m., and then at 8 a.m. the "hallelujahs" from the nearby church commenced. It was a really tough night.

The next morning

Checking e-mails in the lobby of the Tou'Ngou Hotel

We went down for breakfast in the dining room: Petit déjeuner prestige, which meant continental breakfast plus an omelet and yoghurt: a copious breakfast, indeed. There were a few waitresses in the room, all just standing in the corner waiting to be called. There was no initiative, no questions, and no conversation with the patrons.

The hotel had spotty wi-fi so we sat in the very tiny lobby (two armchairs, a love seat, and a desk and chair) to touch bases with our families. *(See page 61 for more about this hotel.)*

Hilton Hotel, Yaoundé

(We didn't stay at the Hilton because of the high rates. We only visited.) We eventually got to the Hilton Hotel. The building looked lackluster and terribly dated and half of the letters of the hotel's name that were blazoned on the façade were missing, which seemed symbolic of the neighborhood. We went to the bar for a beer and here we found a totally different world: well-dressed African businessmen, some in suits, some in traditional clothing—all busy with laptops and cell phones.

The Talotel Hotel, Bafoussam

Hotel - Restaurant -Grill - Service Traiteur - Business Center - Fête & Reunion - Pressing - Excursion
B.P. 110 Bafoussam, Cameroun
Situé 24 Rue derrière la maison du Parti
(The road behind the "Maison du Parti.)
Tel: (237) 344 41 85 / 344 61 81
Fax: (237) 344 43 46
Reservations: (237) 738 96 96 / 999 49 60
E-Mail: talotel@tatotel.com
Site: www.talotel.com
Juliana Wubilla-Yeba, Directrice d'Exploitation
E-mail: julianatalotel@yahoo.com

Outdoor restaurant/bar area of the Talotel Hotel

Our hotel was right across from the central market. It was composed of two buildings—one ultra modern, the other older but renovated. Of course we were in the old building (just like in Yaoundé). The rooms were big with king size beds, a TV, mini bar (not hooked up), a beautiful tiled bathroom with a proper shower and a toilet seat (absent in so many other places). The rooms were about $100 each which was expensive for Cameroon. They had nice marble floors, carved wood doors, a comfortable bed. But the details were still off—lousy colors, peeling paint on the walls. Paul's room had a view of a wall and mine had a view of the adjoining slums.

Later that day

Paul and I met up at the bar (the only one) where we sat in upholstered captain chairs. Paul had a few cocktails and I managed to drink a beer (first thing I had all day). I asked the barman if I could get a few French fries since I hadn't eaten since the day before and at that point it was the only thing appealing to me. We were the only people there, watched the news, and could hear music in the background (Joe le Taxi, Aline, Le Téléphone Pleure, old French tunes from the 80's—like being in a time warp!). Then the news became dramatic: attack in Nairobi in a mall, 87 dead in a Nigerian attack. As my daughter had said, horrible things were happening in the countries neighboring Cameroon. And now the horror seemed everywhere.

The following day

Up early, as usual, since the sun comes up at six and the city streets start being noisy. We went down to breakfast which was a big buffet of unrecognizable meats and grains kept warm in big pans. No thank you. I would not risk that. So I had coffee and a simple pain au chocolat and they charged me for a full breakfast: quite an expensive cup of bad instant coffee. There were no menus or signs with prices and it was always a surprise, even in a supposedly nice hotel like this which catered to lots of business travelers.

Before even going to breakfast we asked the director of the hotel to get us a driver. The car would be a RAV4 and the driver would cost 60,000 CFA plus the price of gas. He didn't arrive until 10:30, a good hour later than expected. He filled up the tank which was a big mistake. It cost us 30,000 CFA (about $60, more than I pay in expensive Los Angeles). The trip we wanted only took about ¼ of a tank. I hated being taken for a piggy bank. He should have been more honest on that one.

That evening

Back to the hotel to freshen up a bit and downstairs at 6 p.m. to check family e-mails and have a beer. There was no WiFi at the bar, only at the reception, where the only place to sit was on two small chairs in a corner.

Check-out

Checking out of what was supposed to be the swankiest hotel in Bafoussam was an unforgettable experience. The director was a real wheeler-dealer and wanted Euros (in cash) to pay the hotel bill, or at least CFA. I told her that we didn't have that much cash on us and when we made the reservation we specified that we wanted to pay by credit car. It was, after all a big hotel bill. She grudgingly relented and accepted the card for the 300,000 CFA bill. But for the transportation costs (two days for the visits to Bamenda and Foumban, which came to 60,000 CFA a day, transportation to Kribi for 70,000 plus gas and the hotel for the driver) she wanted only cash. As she said "une affaire de comptabilité" (an accounting issue). More like "détournement de fonds" (misappropriation of funds)! So I dove into my sock and extracted the wallet strapped around my ankle and gave her $760 for the various transportation costs. Her exchange rate had been, naturally, disastrous.

(Go to page 128 for more information about this hotel.)

Hotel Rim Touristique, Bafia

Located in the Administrative section of the city across from the municipal soccer field and the weekly outdoor market
Director: Mr. Rim
Tel: (237) 22 28 50 53 / 99 53 96 99

We found the Hotel Rim Touristique, a nice looking new building ... I asked to see the owner. We had to wait but it was worth it. Mr. Rim was very polite and welcoming. He was furious that our reservation had not been written down when I called in June. He told his employees that he was unhappy about a total lack of professionalism, grabbed the reservation sheets ... and started moving people around. He found us two rooms, clean and spacious, beautiful wooden inlay on the ceilings, a big bed, bathroom with the hole in the floor for the shower, only cold water. Now that was the Bafia that I remembered: cold, brownish water.

Darleen and Mr. Rim.

We asked if there was some food at the hotel. There was no real restaurant but they could grill us some chicken and we had beers (nutritious and a good way to stay hydrated). The hotel employee who had been copiously berated at that morning for not properly noting reservations found out that my brother liked safou and went across the road to the outdoor market to buy some for him. She grilled them and they were delicious: very tart and sweet at the same time. The skin was thick and the seed was big but the small quantity of flesh was really lovely to eat. But with any exotic fruit, they were to be enjoyed in moderation.

The next day

Up early. The sun was up at six a.m. as were the roosters who serenaded outside my window. We went outside to the "eating area": a few small tables and plastic chairs set up next to the charcoal pit, where the laundry was hanging on the line, and the buckets of water used for washing sheets and dishes were on the ground. A truly multi-purpose area! We ordered breakfast and were surprised to get an omelet with bread and coffee. The omelet had peppers, onions and sardines in it. It was surprisingly good. The coffee was Nescafé (instant and not very good, just like forty years ago). Cameroon was a big producer of coffee beans and obviously it was all exported.

Darleen eathing Safou

The following day

We had wanted to take a nice cold shower and wash a few things in the sink in the brownish water, but our domestic activities were abruptly stopped when the electricity went

Outdoor restaurant area

out (a common occurrence). Forty years ago there was no electricity at all, so even this spotty service was an improvement. We headed to the front of the hotel to watch the outdoor market across the road while it was closing down. Then the generators kicked in and we could enjoy a beer on the terrace, and later head to our rooms for laundry duty, that cold murky shower and an early bedtime. Not much to do in the evening in Bafia; but I was relieved to not have the nightclub noises that had been such a nightmare in Yaoundé. *(Go to page 88 for more information about this hotel.)*

Hotel Les Gîtes de Kribi

Cases, chalets-bungallow, ecologique, herbergement,
salle fitness, restaurant
Direction la Lobe, BP 653, Kribi
Tel: (237) 75 08 08 45 / 77 33 75 28
E-mail: info@kribiholidays.com
www.kribiholidays.com

We found Les Gîtes de Kribi at the edge of town—little bungalows with two bedrooms. We were the only guests at the hotel. Our bungalow had a good sized living room with a sofa and two armchairs which looked soft but had no padding so that you plopped down on

Darleen with Mr. & Mrs. Décieux, the owners of Les Gîtes de Kribi Hotel

Our bungalow

wooden planks rather than the foam cushions of regular sofas. There was a table and a big fridge in the living room. The kitchen was tiny with a small camping stove. Each bedroom had a bathroom. It was clean and spacious enough. The ocean view was a little hard to see behind the dense vegetation but you could hear the ocean which was lovely. A much nicer place than I had expected, which was a relief. We crossed the road to the hotel bar/restaurant which was on the beach. ...We decided to splurge and have dinner at the restaurant. ... Off to bed where the rooms were cooled by the ocean breeze. Divine, again!

(Go to page149 for more information about this hotel and restaurant.)

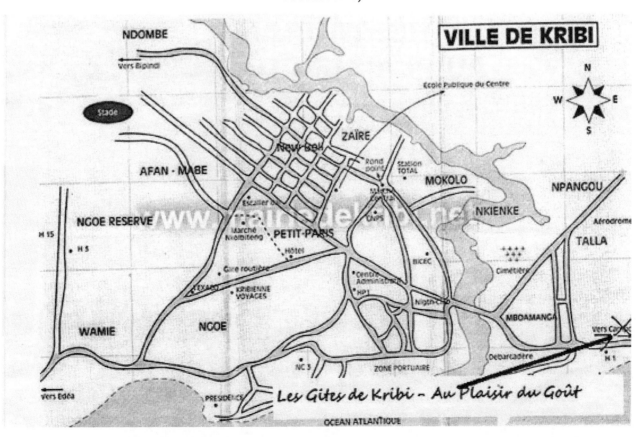

Les Gîtes de Kribi – Au Plaisir du Goût

MONEY

Cameroon uses currency from the Bank of Central African State or CFA. The currency comes in bills of 500, 1000, 5000, and 10000 CFA francs. The 500 CFA bill is being phased out and replaced by a 500 CFA coin. Coins come in dominations of 50, 100, and 500 francs. With all those zeros used on the currency I found an easy way to figure out how CFA translates into dollars. Take the first two numbers of a note of 10,000 francs (10), for example. Then cut that number in half (5), which gives you the amount in dollars. Therefore, 10,000 francs is worth about 5 dollars.

We decided to bring cash because Cameroon currency cannot be exchanged outside of Cameroon. We brought both U.S. dollars and euros in large denominations because smaller bills are difficult to exchange. Keeping large amounts of money is stressful because of the fear of being robbed. We kept our money on our persons at all times. We divided the money so that we kept it in several different places. I kept my dollars in my sock, and the euros were kept in my wallet, which had a thick visible chain attached to my belt to prevent pick-pocketing. Darleen carried money in her totebag with the water bottles and bananas, as well as in an ankle wrap.

We knew that we would be arriving late Saturday night and that it would be Monday morning before we could exchange money. We hoped for the best when we arrived at the airport. After getting our luggage, we asked a security guard about changing money. He made a quick cell phone call, and a money changer appeared almost immediately. We changed enough euros for our taxi ride to our hotel and tips for the security guard and our taxi driver and for our expenses until Monday.

Changing money legally in Cameroon is not easy or fast. Banks don't change money; there are money exchange stores which are not easy to find. We needed photocopies of our passport to change money. It's one of the requirements, so we had copies beforehand to save time and avoid the trouble of finding a place to have a photocopy made.

There are "other ways" to change money. However, it's best to know who you are dealing with. It was risky, but it was fast and easy. We relied on our driver to find us a money changer who offered equal or better rates. Our driver just called ahead, and we drove to a place where we could change money without leaving our car. I found that euros were easier to change and have a greater exchange rate than dollars. (The exchange rate for dollars hovers about 500 francs to the dollar.) Cameroon law states that no more than a few thousand francs can be taken out of the country so before changing our extra CFA francs back into euros or dollars when we left the country, we were sure to keep 5000 francs per person because it is necessary to pay an airport exit fee.

Credit cards can be used in Cameroon, but we were wary about identity theft. Although we didn't want to use any credit cards, I did alert my bank that I was going to Cameroon just in case we needed to use it. I didn't want to take a chance that my card would be blocked. It turned out that I did use my credit card once to pay for our hotel in Bafoussam. I met with the owner of the hotel personally and we carried out the transaction in the privacy of her office. The owner was surprised that there was no security chip that is required with European issued cards. She recommended not using it. As for ATM machines, I did see a few -- mostly at gas stations.

Exchanging Money

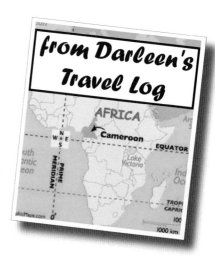

Exchanging Money at the Airport

As we headed out of the baggage area I asked a policeman about exchanging money. He said the bureau was closed (on Saturday evening). Of course! Why have it open when a planeload of people needing CFA (that cannot be bought abroad) arrive? But he knew of someone who could come and exchange some money with better rates than the bank. Of course! Along came a beautiful woman in fine clothes and jewelry carrying a small bag of money. We exchanged 200 Euros but had no idea if the exchange rate was decent. We just needed money at that point to pay a taxi.

Exchanging Money in Bafoussam

We headed back to Bafoussam to change some money at the Exchange Bureau. The process was complicated here because we needed to get photocopies of the passport for the application. No machine at the bureau, of course, but a shop many blocks away could make the copies.

Exchanging Money in Bafia

We headed downtown to change money at the bank. Amazingly enough, the bank didn't have the government's permission to do that and we were sent to an exchange office. There, after filling out a lot of paperwork, we got some CFA at a rate that was close to what we had gotten in the street in Yaoundé.

Grilled fish at Yaya restaurant in Bafia

u and rice Foumban

vacado at the afe de Yaoundé

Chicken & plantain in Banenda

21

FOOD & DRINK

There is a saying that should always be kept in mind: "Cook it, peel it, or forget it." Those who are not careful about what they eat will eventually end up sick. We avoided salads and food made with sauces unless we made them ourselves. So, we ate grilled meat or chicken with roasted plantain or French fries on many occasions. We took along some Imodium just in case. And we actually had one pill at breakfast every day just as a precaution. When traveling and not knowing where our next meal would be, we packed some snack foods in our luggage. I brought several packages of trail mix, nuts, cookies, and beef jerky. They turned out to be extremely useful. In hindsight, I should have brought more with me. When we could not find a restaurant that we liked or while we were on the road travelling around the country, we went to supermarkets, convenience stores, and gas stations where we could buy canned tuna, fresh bread, yogurt, packaged cheese, cookies, biscuits, soft drinks, and other packaged goods.

Bottled water is readily available in all parts of the country. Although running water is available in most hotels, it is recommended not to drink it or use it to brush your teeth. A very popular drink is beer. It is easily available, has a low alcohol content of about 2.5%, and is a source of protein. Hard liquor such as vodka and whisky are also available, but the cost is very high -- about $10 for a Screwdriver (vodka and orange juice). After the shock of our bar bill one evening at our hotel in Bafoussam, we decided to stick to beer for the rest of the trip. Soft drinks in bottles and cans are also widely available.

Salt is sparingly used so bring your own if you need it. We found that bread and pastries have little or no salt and taste a little flat. For seasoning, piment sauce is used and is found everywhere. It's hot, delicious and even a little addictive. Although I'm not a fan of very spicy food, I enjoyed having a little of it with every meal.

< *Chicken at the Hotel Rim Touristique in Bafia*

Shrimp in Kribi

Steak and fries in Yaoundé

Safou

Pasta at the Cafe de Yaounde

Darleen at the Cafe de Yaoundé

DREAMLAND RESTAURANT

MENU

Dreamland is a restaurant in Bamenda

MAIN DISHES

FUFU CORN	Huckleberry	1500F
FUFU CORN	Huckleberry & Khati Khati	2500F
EKWANG		1500F
WATER FUFU/ GARRI	Eru	1500F
GARRI	Okro	2000F
ACHU	Black Sauce	1500F
	Yellow Sauce	1500F
WHITE BEANS	French fries	1500F
BEEF STEW	Plantain fries or french fries	1500F
NDOLE (BEEF)	Rice	2000F
	Yams	2000F
	Fried Plantain	3500F
NDOLE (CHICKEN)		3500F
¼ CHICKEN		2500F
¼ CHICKEN & MUSHROOM	French fries	3500F
¼ CHICKEN, BEANS VEGETABLE	Plantain fries Rice	3000F
½ CHICKEN DG	Yams	4500F
FULL CHICKEN DG		8000F
WHITE PEPPER STEAK		2500F
GREEN PEPPER STEAK		2500F
STEAK MUSHROOM		3500F
STEAK MOUTARDE		3500F
SPAGHETTIS BOLOGNAISE		3500F
GRILLED CHEESE		1500F
CHOW MEIN VEGETARIAN	Egg. Spaghetti	1500F
CHOW MEIN	Egg, spaghetti, beef	2000F
A MIXED PLATE	Rice huckleberry or beans	1500F
A MIXED PLATE	At Chef's Disposition	2500F
LIVER AND TOWEL PEPPER SOUP/SHRIMPS	Yams	2000F
FOOT COW PEPPER SOUP	Fried Plantains	2000F
CHICKEN PEPPER SOUP	Rice	2500F
BAR FISH PEPPER SOUP		3000F

SELF SERVICE (BUFFET)

WEEK DAYS 12:00 Noon - 4:00 PM

3.000FRS Only !

PIMENTSAUCE

Piment sauce is found on every table

CAMEROONIAN BEERS

Guinness Foreign Extra Stout	Foreign Stout
Satzenbrau	Pale Lager
Beaufort 8.9	Strong Pale Lager
Beaufort (Cameroon)	Pale Lager
33 Export (Cameroon)	Pale Lager
Mützig (Cameroon)	Pale Lager
Kadji Beer Blonde	Pale Lager
Isenbeck Premium (Cameroon)	Czech Pilsner (Světlý)
Castel Beer (Cameroon)	Pale Lager

RESTAURANT REVIEWS

Bois Sainte Anastasie Restaurant, Yaoundé

12567 Rue Sebastien Essomba
Tel.: (237) 22 05 48 22

Bois Sainte Anastie Restaurant is a buffet with a beautiful botanical garden around it. The food was cheap for us and very mild. The main problem being we had no idea what most of it was: different meat or fish dishes in sauce, or vegetables that I had never seen before. The beer on the menu: 33 Export, which we knew well.. We walked around the gardens after lunch. They were surprising and lovely and cost 1000 CFA ($2) to visit, which eliminated a large swath of the population. The people roaming the gardens were well-dressed and taking time on a Sunday to rest. Not like in the other neighborhoods where everyone was working.

Café de Yaoundé Restaurant, Yaoundé

Le Cafe de Yaoundé Restaurant, Avenue Churchill, **(237)** 22 22 85 94

Our driver took us to a restaurant that he said was for "white people", Le Café de Yaoundé, run by an Italian. It was in an old house with a huge terrace, surrounded by lush gardens. And yes, lots of "white" people inside, plus some Cameroonian businessmen. Beautiful décor, paintings on the wall, lovely batik linen, delicious food: we were stunned. A perfect place and a good meal for 21000 CFA for two (about $40): pricey for Cameroon, affordable for us.

(A few days later)

After all the wonderful shopping we had our driver take us to have lunch at the Café de Yaoundé which was an absolute oasis. Paul had the "Château Briant" (loved the spelling) and I had the fresh tagliatelli with fresh ginger. We shared a crème caramel. Delicious food and such a lovely garden to look at. A group of Spaniards came in for lunch. I hadn't seen so many Europeans in the same place since we arrived. We lingered over lunch as long as possible and then asked if we could sit in the garden to wait for our driver. Response: "Il n'y a pas de souci" (no problem), which people seemed to say a lot in Cameroon. We sat amongst the flowers and it was very peaceful.

The Italian owner came out to talk to us and asked us if we would like a limoncello. Of course, even though I had no idea what he was offering. It turned out to be a liqueur made with lemons that was really delicious. Our last real meal of the day and it was exquisite.
(Go to pages 85 for more information about this restaurant.)

ETS Yaya Restaurant, Bafia

La Maison des Oeufs et du Vin, Cave du Mbam, Restaurant, Situé a cote de Quifeurou, Bafia Tel: (237) 77 63 32 67 or 22 05 82 90

We had a quick lunch at a restaurant recommended by the hotel owner called "Yaya's". It was almost impossible to find since there was no sign whatsoever and it was located in a part of town with a permanent central market full of dilapidated stalls and teeming with people. I would not have ventured into that market for anything! So we had a lunch of fried fish, chicken and fried plantain sitting on a sort of porch watching people use the wall across the alley as a public urinal. Amazing. *(Go to page 102 for more information about this restaurant.)*

Dreamland Restaurant, Bamanda

Commercial Avenue P.O. Box 417
Mankon-Bamenda, Bamenda, Cameroon
Tel.: (237) 33 36 17 00

We asked to be taken to the Dreamland restaurant that had been recommended in the guidebook. It looked decent with big round balconies and private tables. He sat us at a table for ten—there was a view of the street below and fresh air. The temperatures in Bamenda were cooler because of the altitude and the fact it was the rainy season. There was no steak at the market that day so we had chicken and fries. No more sauces for a while! And the ubiquitous beer. *(Go to page 137 for more information about this restaurant.)*

24

Restaurant Tata Mimi, Foumban

Petit dejeuner, touts lets africains et occidentaux,
Tel.: (237) 97 81 88 53

The driver asked around and took us to Tata Mimi's, which had a nice little garden. We were the only clients. There was only one dish on the menu so we took our lives into our hands and ordered that. It turned out to be a tasty beef dish in a palm oil sauce. *(Go to page 143 for more information about this restaurant.)*

Le Plaisir du Gôut Restaurant-Bar-Café, Kribi

(at the Gîte de Kribi Hotel, Kribi) Contact: 33 46 18 21 or 75 08 08 45
Vers les Chutes de la Lobé en face Les Gîtes de Kribi • Email: restaurant@auplaisirdugout.com • www. auplaisirdugout.com

We crossed the road to the hotel bar/restaurant which was on the beach. This place was brand new and beautifully decorated—more like Hawaii or the Caribbean. We sat on the terrace, which was literally on the sand and had beers. I told Paul that I felt like I had died and gone to heaven. He answered that maybe we did die on that road and this was heaven! We just sat there stunned by the beauty of the beach, the breeze, the extraordinary sunset. This felt cleansing after so many days in hot, dusty towns teeming with humanity.

We decided to splurge and have dinner at the restaurant. I had shrimp flambé au whisky and Paul had the chicken in peanut sauce that he remembered so well. We shared an appetizer, chutney d'avocat (avocado, apple, shrimp, and lettuce in a thin sauce) and a bottle of Cabernet d'Anjou. Divine!

The next day

We went to the bar and watched the sunset, which was spectacular, and even had cocktails. We thought we would splurge since we were cooking our own dinner. Paul had a screwdriver and I had a Tequila Sunrise, complete with umbrella and slice of tomato. Paradise. We sat there for a long time talking about our adventures and had a second cocktail. The cook came out and asked us to try his pizza. The restaurant was planning on serving it and he was perfecting his dish. It was good but not spicy enough, which was surprising considering the traditional spices they use in Cameroon. ... Our waitress was very sweet and told us about her nine year old hyperactive son Brian and her life. We were the only customers there and it was lovely to be able to talk with the employees about Cameroon and learn about their lives. *(Go to page 154 for more information about this restaurant.)*

La Marina de Kribi

Pizzeria, Bar-Restaurant - Port de Plaisance
B.P. 628 Kribi, Cameroun
Tel: (237) 94 76 74 34 / 97 78 69 48 / 71 53 37 97
E-mail: marinadekribi@yahoo.fr

We walked all the way to the marina, went into a bar there and, of course, had a beer. It was only 10:30 a.m., but it was hot and this was Africa. We watched the pirogues coming in with the day's catch of fish and shrimp. *(Go to page 156 for more information about this restaurant.)*

Outdoor patio of the Marina Restaurant

Marina Restaurant

View of Kribi from the Marina Restaurant

Expresso House, Yaoundé

Carefour Bastos

... At 3:30 our driver arrived and we asked him to take us to the Bastos neighborhood for a coffee. He brought us to a trendy café that he thought we would like. It was full of young Cameroonians, rich, entitled, snobbish, dressed in fashionable clothes and harboring an attitude of languorous boredom. They were the moneyed leisure class. ... What was there to do in Yaoundé? No cinemas, concerts, parks, only a few cafés and night clubs. It seemed like a golden prison. We had a couple of bad coffees. My espresso was transparent with a little foam on top. Ah! We sat in the lounge area and relaxed, buying more time.

CLOTHING

Cameroonians dress fairly conservatively. In the cities men wear short-sleeved shirts with long pants, which often are made of the same material. Business men and office workers wear suits. Men from the north of the country often wear long flowing robes. Young men's clothes are more fashionable than the older generations and resemble what youth of the same age wear around the world.

Women dress modestly and many wear western-style dresses, blouses with skirts, or colorful native clothing. Bold cloth patterns can be see everywhere. Muslim women wear long and often very colorful robes with head scarves.

Shorts are not usually worn in public except by the younger generations. The only time I felt comfortable wearing shorts was in Kribi while walking along the beach, as well as in town. Being used to westerners, the residents of Kribi seem to accept a more laid-back dress code. We brought light wrinkle-free clothing. I took six short-sleeve shirts and three pairs of pants, a pair of shorts, a light jacket, one long sleeve dress shirt and one pair of black slacks for more formal occasions. Other items that I brought were a hat, sunglasses, a light coat that could double as a rain coat, and a small umbrella. In order to make more room for the purchases we were planning to make, I took old underwear and socks, which I threw away instead of bringing back home with me.

Sandals are common, but for extensive walking, we wore covered shoes because most streets and sidewalk surfaces are uneven. Also, when we walked in the bush, we didn't want to make our feet vulnerable to fire ant bites, for example. In case we wanted to do some clothes washing in our hotel room, we brought a small bottle of liquid detergent. I used it twice; Darleen used it more often.

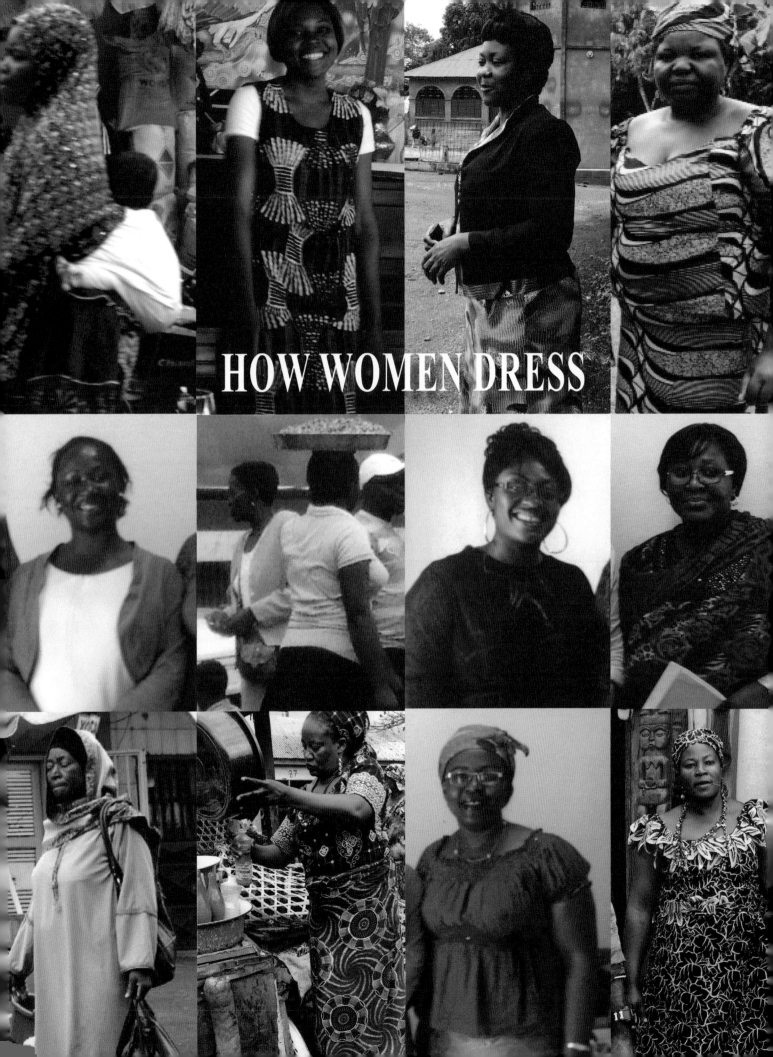

HOW WOMEN DRESS

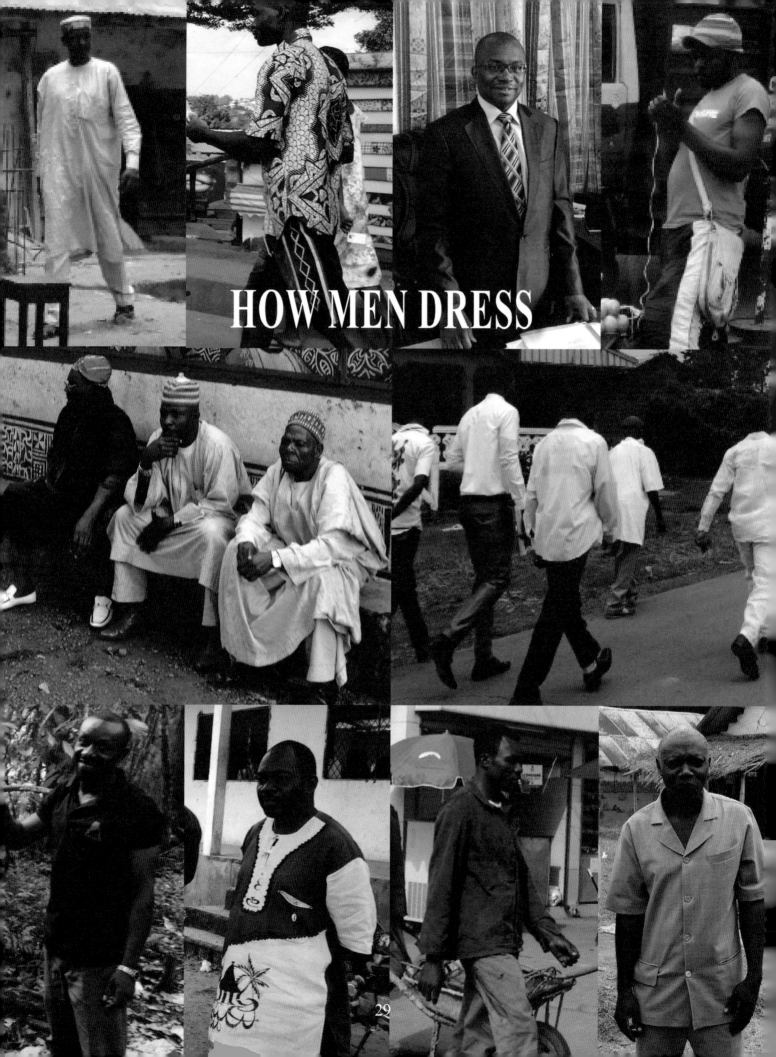

HOW MEN DRESS

SHOPPING

When we knew what we wanted to buy--a cell phone, for example--we asked our driver to take us to a place he was familiar with or had him call someone he knew. Shopping in a store is very straight forward and similar to shopping in the U.S. and Europe. We took along the usual toiletries: tooth brush and tooth paste, a bar of soap, hand sanitizer, and small bottles of body wash and shampoo. Soap was available at our hotels, but complementary bottles of body wash, shampoo, hair conditioner, and body lotion/moisturizer were not. These items are easily available throughout Cameroon, but we wanted to bring brands that we were familiar with, and we didn't want to spend time shopping for these items. Baby wipes are also useful for those moments when toilet paper is not available.

When visiting an open market, we were prepared to be approached, beckoned, pestered, and sometimes harassed. It may be stressful, but shoppers are expected to bargain for everything. My approach was to ask the price of an item, offer to pay a third of the asking price, and negotiate until the price is 50%. If it was something I really wanted, I knew that might have to pay a little more. Sometimes I didn't bother to bargain for prices at all, especially at outdoor food markets because the prices were already low. When buying souvenirs, travelers need to be aware that some cultural items sold in artisan shops may be taxed at the airport on your way home. During the customs check leaving the airport we were asked if we had bought any souvenirs and what kind. Travelers should be prepared to pay a tax for such things as wood carvings, jewelry, leather goods, batik cloth and other hand-crafted items. We declared nothing. The inspectors didn't open our bags, and sent us on our way.

Clothing shop in Bafia

SHOPPING

Shopping for Cloth in Yaoundé

NEW17-LAKING DETAIL YAOUNDE (Cloth Store) • *237) 99 91 30 54

... Then off to a proper store—with price tags! We hadn't seen that yet. We found some lovely pagnes, priced right (buy 3 get a 4th free). They were about 6,200 CFA, quite different from the exorbitant prices we had found in Foumban. We saw the luxury waxed pagnes we had paid 20,000 CFA for (the shopkeeper had wanted 65,000 CFA). Here they were priced at 14,000. Had we known! But I was pleased to finally have some gorgeous fabric to bring home and offer. We resisted buying the "Teacher's Pagne", a special bolt of cloth with "professeur" written all over it decorated with images of classroom objects. It seems the teachers fashion their uniforms out of this.

Shopping for Food for a Picnic

We went to a grocery store/bakery (in Bafia) to get something for lunch ... So we found some odds and ends: thon (tuna) à la Catalane in a can, Kiri cheese, bread, yoghurt, galettes bretonnes, water. Things we knew wouldn't hurt us too badly. Back to the hotel where Mr. Rim (the owner) said that there was no problem having a picnic on the upper terrace part of the bar: "Vous êtes chez vous ici" (Make yourselves at home). The gentleman knows how to treat his clients. They even brought us plates and utensils along with our beers and we had a lovely picnic.

The Artisanat Section of Yaoundé

There were ... forty stalls manned by some very aggressive and hungry salesmen, and we were the only tourists. There were leather goods ... masks, statues, beads, silver objects and some material. It was a little frightening the way they corralled us around and thrust things in our faces imploring us to buy what they said was the best in town, the cheapest, and the rarest. Knowing that antiques cannot leave the country, buying any of it could lead to potential problems. But most of the sculptures were too big or, as far as the masks and small statues were concerned, we had already brought back enough forty years before.

On our last day in Yaounde

Our driver took us shopping. We went back to the artisan center which had a lot more activity than the last time. We bought a few wallets and I found the batik tablecloth that I wanted, having seen it at the Café de Yaoundé. I found a few silver/nickel bracelets that would make nice gifts.

Buying a Cell Phone in Yaoundé

Romulad Electronique (Electronics Store) • Vente, Telephones portables et Accessories
Situé a la deccents NIKI Marache Central face MAHAL Couloir) et en face orange. B.P Yaoundé (237)
93 87 31 18 • (We bought a Nukia cell phone 1280 (No 6942) for 10,000 CFA.)

Our driver told us that we should have a cell phone to call him when we wanted to be picked up and when we needed to contact our friends. So instead of going into a store, we drove down a very crowded street near the central market, and stayed in the back seat while a "friend" brought us a cell phone. ... A few minutes later we stopped to buy some minutes. Another "friend" that our driver beckoned jumped into the front seat and sold us the SIM card. All without leaving the back seat of the car. And we were even warned by Dieudonné that it wouldn't be prudent to do business in the street. It was all so different from the way I was used to shopping that I felt a bit lost.

Shopping in Foumban

Foumban outdoor market

In Foumban we asked our driver to take us to the Village of Artisans where there were no artisan studios in sight, only small stalls called "galleries," all selling the same masks and statues. I found a few brass bracelets and had to bargain. The prices they asked for were really ridiculous, even more than what I could afford to pay in the United States. We were seen as "tourists-rich" so they tried to get as much as they could out of us. We were swarmed by the merchants—come and see my shop, I have the best prices, I have antiques that I can offer you at special prices. We certainly didn't want to buy any masks; we had bought those years ago. We expressed an interest in pagnes (bolts of colorful cloth). A veritable cohort of merchants took us to the market place for material. A lot of the same— heavy embroidered tablecloths, pagnes that were not as nice as before, some even made of polyester. The market had wide enough alleys so it wasn't too frightening. We stuck close to our driver. I managed to take a few pictures, but barely. The only two tourists in the entire market—how was that for a bull's eye? We found two pagnes that we liked. The merchant wanted 65,000 CFA. I offered 20,000. Even the equivalent of $40 was a lot. Everything was overpriced. But then again we were the miracle tourists who suddenly appeared out of nowhere.

Foumban's Village of Artisans

Shopping at the Fish Market in Kribi

We could see a decent embarcadero/fish market (built by the Japanese, we learned) (from the Marina Restaurant) and went down to buy something for dinner. There were big slabs of concrete in the embarcadero where we could see all kinds of fish and shellfish—bass, shark, shrimp, gambas, crayfish, lobster, squid. We walked all around amazed at the variety and freshness—of course, it was all freshly caught and still alive! We decided to have gambas and lobster for dinner (at $10 a pound) and shrimp for the next evening. Then we went through the small town to the vegetable market. The alleys were wider than in Bafia or Bafoussam and it felt more comfortable to do some shopping—tomatoes, garlic, onions, parsley, basil.

MAJOR CHANGES

The governmental administrative center of Yaoundé

I was very eager to see how life had changed in Cameroon. For years I could not find much information. News was very limited, except for the occasional news story. Gradually, with the advent of the Internet, email, blogs, YouTube, and Pocket Tunes, more information became available. More and more I was able to read articles, see current photos and video clips, view TV shows, listen to music and radio programs, and even contact individuals. In 2006, I contacted Kelly McPheerson, a Peace Corps volunteer in Bafia. She contacted the director of my former school in Bafia by email and arranged for a school-to-school and pen-pal relationship between Fairfax High School/Adult School in Los Angeles and the

Left: The tallest building in Yaoundé in 1971
Right: the same building in 2013

Lycée de Bafia. The students at Fairfax High School/ Adult School raised $1,800 to fund the first summer school Internet course. I sent the money to Kelly, and she organized the summer school program. This activity was my first real contact with Cameroon since I left in 1972.

Although I was able to "reconnect" and learn more about how life had been transformed in Cameroon over the last ten years, I wanted to see the changes for myself. To record these changes, I kept a notebook with me to record my thoughts and feelings about what I saw, heard, and read during my trip. After reviewing my notes, here's my list of what I consider are the twelve major changes that have taken place over the past four decades.

CELL PHONES & ELECRICITY

I believe the single biggest change is the ability to communicate with one another by cell phone throughout the country. Forty years ago, having a telephone was a rarity limited to cities. Today, it seems that everyone has a cell phone -- even in the smallest villages in remote areas. Orange is the country's cell-phone provider and its bright orange sign can be seen everywhere. Travelling around the countryside, one commonly saw tall communication towers. Wifi is available, but not to the extent it is in Europe or the U.S. It can be found in hotels and in internet cafés, which are popping up everywhere. During my trip, I saw some businessmen and professionals in the hotels using smart phones, tablets, and laptops. However, I did not see them being used elsewhere.

Years ago, access to electricity was limited to big cities; today, even medium size towns have electricity, even though there may be frequent outages. As an example, electricity came to Bafia in the mid-2000s. While traveling around the country, I saw many tall towers carrying high-tension wires crossing the country.

Similar relay towers are seen all over the country.

Orange is the country's cell phone provider.

Satellite dishes and wires are everywhere

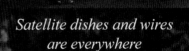

A store front cell phone ad in Yaoundé. 34

EDUCATION

When I taught in Cameroon, there few schools; today there are schools all over the country, even in the smallest villages. The topic of instruction is close to my heart because I have been an educator all of my professional life. I have had experience being an ESL instructor in Cameroon, Zaire (Congo), and Los Angeles; an author of a dozen ESL textbooks; a school principal for the Los Angeles Unified School District, and an instructor at the American Language Center at UCLA Extension.

I was anxious to see how the school system had changed after so many years. I was fortunate to visit five schools: Lycée Bilingue de Bafia, Lycée Classique de Bafia, Lycée de Donenkeng, the Donenkeng Pre-school, and the Catholic Pre-school at Gondon in Bafia. Darleen brought dolls, teddy-bears, and dresses for the pre-schoolers. I brought school supplies for the lycée students. The supplies were donated by friends and included pencils, pens, stickers, and toothbrushes.

A typical school day at the Lycée of Donenkeng

THE FUTURE OF CAMEROON

Although my "surprise" school visits were short, I did manage to get a sense of how schools are faring. The biggest change I noticed was the number of schools that I saw. They are everywhere and are visible along every road I was on. As an example, in 1969 Bafia had one lycée that could not accommodate all secondary school students, so there were rigorous entrance exams to select the "crème de la crème" and the most affluent students who had "connections." Today, there are three different public lycées as well as a Catholic one.

The first German school in Douala around 1900 (Photo from a school textbook "Histoire du Cameroon," 1960)

Although I saw many more school buildings, they appeared little different from those of decades ago. The average school consists of a few classroom buildings without electricity in a small compound with a playground and/or soccer field. School buildings are constructed of concrete walls and floor, an aluminum roof, and open windows with an occasional screen. The typical classroom consist of nothing more than a teacher; a blackboard; a teacher's table; and too few, well-worn, wooden desks and benches to accommodate too many students. Students wear colored uniforms that vary from school to school.

While speaking to administrators and teachers, I was

A billboard for a private technical school in Bamenda

not surprised to learn that some of them could not talk about their schools' history because they had been recently transferred and were not familiar with their new school and communities. As it was when I taught in Cameroon, teachers and school administrators are part of a highly centralized system and are frequently transferred to other parts of the country.

Lack of security of the school buildings at night seems to be a major issue since there are few fences, and the classrooms are easily accessible through open windows, especially in rural areas. The only classroom I saw that had educational material displayed and stored around the classroom was at the Catholic pre-school at Gondon in Bafia. A pre-school teacher at Donenkeng told me that she had to take all school materials and supplies home every night because of the constant break-ins. The only educational materials I saw in the public schools were the students' personal textbooks, notebooks, pencils, pens, and nothing more.

Though I didn't visit any private schools, I did see many billboards advertising technical schools, especially computer technology.

DONENKENG PRE-SCHOOL

*A typical school day at a
pre-school of Donenkeng*

A Visit to Two Pre-Schools
École Maternelle Donenkeng

from Darleen's Travel Log

... Then we went to a pre-school (Ecole Maternelle Donenkeng) which was a few minutes away (from the Presbyterian Mission Hospital) by car. There we met the school's director, Mme. Marie-Claire Atoua, and I explained that I wanted to give dolls and teddy bears and a few dresses to the children, but I didn't have enough for all. (The school was run by the Director, Mme. Atoua Marie Chaire, Directorice de l"Ecole Maternelle de Donenkeng Tel: (237) 99 33 73 63 or 70 58 41 17 • (Instructors: Ambadiang Balbine et Natoume Ngada Sophie • Maitresses Petite Section)

I was an "Ambassador" for *Dollies Making A Difference* (a group of women in Pacific Palisades, CA who made cloth dolls by hand to be distributed to children in need in hospitals, orphanages and schools around the world) and for Little Dresses for Africa (a group of women in Carpinteria, CA who made dresses out of donated pillowcases and trim).

We were brought to the class for the youngest children 'la petite section". There had to be at least 50 children (three to four years old) in that classroom. They were absolutely adorable, dressed in little green smocks, the little girls with braided hair. The teacher had the brilliant idea of keeping the dolls in the classroom for all of the children to play with. She would take them home at night because there were no windows and the vandals would steal them. I told her I would like to take some pictures of the children holding the dolls. She had 40 little ones come up (only those wearing the school uniform— the green smocks), and I gave away 20 dolls. Paul took pictures of the distribution, then group shots of the teacher, the children and me. The children were so grateful and happy to have such lovely toys. I could explain in French why I didn't have enough for everyone and why they needed to share the dolls in the classroom. I felt a little like Santa Claus (or rather, Mrs. Claus). I also gave the smallest pillowcase dresses to the teacher to give later to the neediest. It was satisfying to bring them nice things, especially after yesterday when I thought no one wanted them. I was aware that the gifts were small, but they went directly to the kids. *(Read more on page 110.)*

École Maternelle of the Catholic Mission in Bafia

Then we raced off to the Catholic Mission (in Bafia) to see the director of the pre-school, Sister Adèle-Victor. (Sister Adele-Victor Ngo Makee, Pre-school director at the Catholic Mission in Bafia, Tel (237) 99 92 74 47 or 78 18 46 23, E-mail: macacos@camnet.cm)

She was ... smiling and open, and agreed with the ... idea of donating the dolls for the classroom. We went to the "petite section" where there must have been 100 children and two teachers. I was amazed how they could handle so many little ones in one room. Some were crying, and the noise level was, naturally a bit louder. I re-explained to the teachers, Balbine Ambadiang and Sophie Natoume-

Ngada, what I wanted to do and they were thrilled. They had few toys in the room, and what they did have, was worn out and sad looking.

These dolls and teddy bears literally brightened up the room with color. I was told that the problem with donations was that they sometimes end up being sold at the outdoor markets. If the family is struggling they will sell anything to get some money to buy food. I was only hoping the teachers wouldn't get that idea. ... We went back to the Sister's office where I gave her the dresses to be given to needy children at Christmas. A French coopérant had given her clothes for little boys, so this would complement that donation perfectly. She offered us Coke and cookies, which was a blessing after a morning of digestive difficulties. ... It all turned out well in the end. I was happy to make the donations and in the process we met some kind and interesting people.

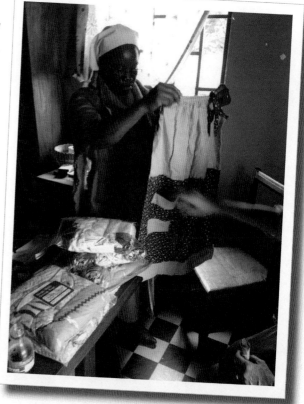

(Read more on page 112.)

HEALTH CARE

Health care seems to have improved greatly. There are now many hospitals and clinics. Years ago, evidence of polio was widespread. The sight of people struggling to walk with single long walking sticks or crutches was common; during this trip, I saw only two people struggling with a wheelchair. In addition, people seemed to be well-fed and in good health. Years ago I saw malnourished children with red

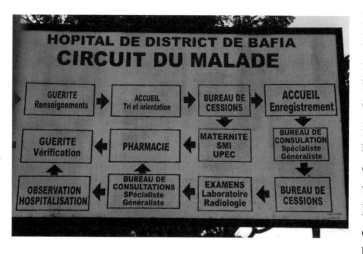

hair and extended bellies. During this trip, I didn't see any of that. Food seemed to be plentiful. I saw many outdoor markets that were full of fruit, vegetables, and meat. The only time I heard of malnourished children was from our driver in Kribi. He said that the only case of malnutrition he knew about was in villages of Nigerian fishermen who lived in isolation along the coast north of Kribi.

Bafia Hospital

Murals on the walls of the radiology building at the Presbyterian Hospital at Donenkeng

A Visit to the Presbyterian Mission Hospital at Donenkeng

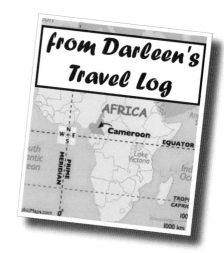

from Darleen's Travel Log

Darleen and Dr. Mgengang

... We headed out to Donenken, the Presbyterian Mission (Hospital). This was on the old road to Yaounde: paved only for a short time in Bafia, then the old washboard "piste" we knew so well since this was all we had forty years before. Red dusty roads, very narrow, bordered with lush greenery and dotted with shacks. After about 6 km we arrived at the compound. We found the Reverend's house, but he was in the shower and would join us later. We walked over to look at the Sandilands' (a former American doctor) house which was now a complete ruin. The walls and roof were there but everything was covered in mold, overgrown with vegetation, and obviously had been neglected for a long time. It had been a tidy little house, where they had raised their children while they worked at the hospital, complete with flowers and a lawn. After Dr. Sandilands left, the mission compound was bought by the state and the missionaries couldn't keep it up. Donations from the church dwindled and without funds the slow process of decay began. Paul was visibly disappointed.

Then we went to the hospital—same buildings, only now, they too were crumbling. We spoke with the head nurse who told us about the problems to get supplies and medicine. It was very sad to see that the life's work of Dr. and Mrs. Sandilands was reduced to this. The Presbyterian mission built everything, ran it for twenty-five years, trained nurses, and provided vital medical help. Once the doctor left, it slowly disintegrated. It seemed to be a combination of lack of funds and know how, and the paralysis that sets in when things stop working. *(Read more about Donenkeng on page 104.)*

Operating Room

The road between Yaoundé and Bafia in 2013

ROADS

The roads had dramatically improved. Then, there were few paved roads; today most major cities (except in the extreme north of the country) are connected by a network of paved toll roads and bridges. Although most major highways are good, the worst road we experienced was between Basoussam and Bamenda. It was full of pot holes and ruts. Tolls cost 500 francs (about $1.00) for every 50 miles or so. Years ago, road accidents were common; today, there are fewer accidents due to inspection road blocks that enforce weight limits and the use of seatbelts. Additionally, there are countless speed bumps that force drivers to reduce their speed. Apparently, it's working. I know because I got a 5000 franc ticket at one of these checkpoints for not wearing my seat belt. A big change that surprised me was the number of modern gas stations that are located along major highways. They are a good place to shop for snacks, bottled water, and the use of restrooms while traveling. I had thought that gas would be cheap, but it wasn't. The cost is about the same as in the United States.

The road between Yaoundé and Bafia in 1969

RELIGION

Religion is a major driving force in Cameroon. Christian dominations make us the largest group, followed by Muslims and animists. I am not a religious person and do not belong to any church. I am not used to being bombarded with relition. What surprised me was the number of churches and mosques there are compared to 43 years ago. The Catholic Church is a major influence and has missions in every part of the country. Again, to use Bafia as an example, the archdiocese has expanded tremendously with the building of a new cathedral, schools, and community center surrounded by a supporting community of clergy, teachers, and lay people in their own neighborhood in the Gundun area of town. I met with Bishop Bala in Bafia and had a very nice conversation about the mission and its good works and outreach into the community. I left his office very impressed.

Another prominent Christian organization is the Presbyterian Church, which has played a major role in Cameroonian history by providing medical clinics throughout the county, especially in the east, center and south of the country. Whereas Catholicism has grown, Presbyterianism seems to have waned due to reduced donations from other countries, as I was told by a doctor at a Presbyterian mission hospital.

I came across a number of evangelical preachers. They preach on the streets, on television, and in small neighborhood churches. The ones I encountered were loud and annoying. For example, screaming and yelling from loudspeakers coming from a preacher at a small assembly late into the night kept me from sleeping. What I could make out was that he was a healer casting out the devil. This particular preacher was telling his followers to accept their lot in life and that there is no way out except if it's God's will. Wouldn't this drain their sense of personal responsibility, limit their creativity, discourage them from thinking for themselves to solve their own problems, and make them dependent on religion? You might think that a country like Cameroon, which has one of the highest literacy rates in Africa, would produce more "rational" people who can see through these individuals who use their religious beliefs as a business to raise money, gain power, and stroke their own egos. This is where,

*A Baptist church
in Yaoundé*

The Catholic Cathedral in the Gondon neighborhood of Bafia

I believe, the anti-gay sentiments come from, that is to say, imported western religions, and not from African culture.

I did not discuss the topic of homosexuality during my trip, not knowing what I would find. However, I did watch a debate on television between a social worker and an evangelical religious leader. The social worker calmly argued that gays should be treated with dignity and granted basic human rights, while the preacher espoused his religious beliefs that condemn homosexuality. I came away from the debate saddened that the issue has become not only a religious one, but also a highly emotional one that can trigger hatred and and even violence. I kept thinking how fortunate I was to live in West Hollywood, California, where I do not have to deal with the fear of religious bigotry and violence. Cameroon, as well as,

The Presbyterian church in Donenkeng was build in 1935.

many other countries in Africa, has a long road ahead in extending "real" human rights to all of their citizens. Here's another example of what happens when beliefs trump reason.

Don't get me wrong, there are many good deeds the religious people do, but preaching "love" can be very subjective, apparently.

We did not travel into Muslim areas of the north of the country. However, we did visit Muslim neighborhoods in Yaoundé, Foumban, and Bamenda, in which the main buildings were large beautiful mosques. Even Bafia had an imposing mosque in the center of town. In Yaoundé, it seemed that Muslims keep to themselves and only ventured out of their neighborhoods to work or shop. None of our drivers spoke much about religion. When the topic of religion came up, they shrugged and turned to another subject. The only comment I got was 45 that religion is "big business" in Cameroon.

The main mosque in Bamenda

Mosques in Bafia

46

A Visit with Catholic Bishop Jean-Marie Benoit Bala of Bafia

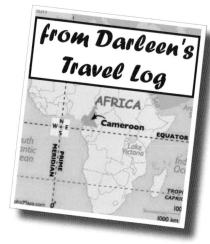

Bishop Bala and Darleen

Tel: (237) 99 41 00 70, Email: jmb-bala@yahoo.fr, mbam-catho@ yahoo.fr

We ... went ... to pay our respects to Bishop Jean-Marie Benoît Bala. I was flabbergasted that he had asked to meet us. News travels fast. He was dressed in a traditional boubou (long tunic worn by African men), sitting at a desk piled high with folders. He was kind and intelligent. Paul gave him one of the laminated bookmarks with an old Cameroonian stamp on it that he had made, which pleased the Bishop very much. He told us about the problems in the parish and an important project helping rehabilitate the young men in the Bafia prison. We even got group pictures. So now we have pictures with Mr. Bidias (former government official), le Préfet, and the Bishop. Only in Bafia! (Read more about our visit on page 112.)

Views of the Catholic Mission at Gondon, Bafia

Catholic Cathedral at the Gondon Mission in Bafia

Centre Paul VI at the Gondon Mission in Bafia

Buildings at the Gondon Missioin in Bafia

Students walking in front of the "Secretariat a l"Education" building

A Visit to the Catholic Cathedral in Yaoundé

He dropped us off at the cathedral. As we walked towards the church where a mass was being held a little girl walking with her mother cried out: "Regarde Maman, les blancs." (Look Mommy, white people). It was then that we realized that we had only seen Cameroonians since our arrival and the neighborhood around the cathedral that we knew well was totally different. We went into the church as the mass was finishing and sat in a pew near the door. When the priest asked the congregation to shake hands with neighbors and wish peace many people came over to us and my brother and I grabbed all the hands that we could—a two-handed greeting and a lovely beginning of our Cameroonian adventure.

Modern toilets are common, but running water isn't.

A bathroom at the Hotel Rim Touristique in Bafia

Rest room at the Mefou Primate Santuary

CLEAN WATER & SANITATION

When I lived in Cameroon, there were few toilets; today there are many more; however, most are without toilet seats! I guess if you've never had a toilet seat, you don't miss it. Where there is no running water, there are barrels of water with buckets for flushing. The best public toilets I found were at the newer gas stations in Yaoundé and along the major highways.

Access to clean water has improved. Years ago, plastic water bottles were non-existent, and water had to be filtered and boiled. It was a long and tedious process. Today, it seems that everyone is drinking water from clear plastic bottles. One negative aspect of this improvement is the eyesore of plastic bottles and bags littered along roads, in gullies, and in garbage piles.

Years ago, women and children carrying water buckets on their heads was an ordinary sight; today, wells with electric pumps and people using them are visible along most major highways.

Although carrying heavy loads on one's head is still a common sight, I didn't see many people carrying buckets of water during my trip.

A water tower at the Hotel Les Gites in Kribi

BILLBOARD

Advertising is alive and well. Here's a sampling.

GOVERNMENT & POLITICS

I avoided talking openly about politics because I didn't know how people would react. However, I did get a sense of what people were thinking. I didn't perceive any overt dislike for the current government. Instead, I detected apathy and disinterest. We arrived just before parliamentary and municipal elections. We saw the candidates' posters, listened to political reports on television, heard blaring ads from loudspeakers positioned on cars and trucks, and witnessed a few street rallies of candidates' supporters. What I sensed was little interest from the general public.

During a visit with newly arrived Peace Corps trainees, I attended a talk on the government structure of Cameroon, which has changed greatly since independence. In brief, Kamerun, a former German colony before World War I, was divided between Great Britain and France and became protectorates. The British protectorate was called "The Cameroons" and the French protectorate was "Cameroun." In 1960, there was a referendum in the Cameroons to determine if the protectorate would join Cameroun to become a new

A sign displayed on the steps in front of a house in Kribi

nation. Part of the British protectorate chose to join the "Republique du Cameroun" (i.e. also referred to as the Republic of Cameroon), and the northern section voted to become part of Nigeria. West Cameroon, the English-speaking part of the country, and the French-speaking part formed a new country in which both parts would be equal partners. Even the Cameroon flag showed two stars to symbolize this partnership. Unique to Africa, it became the only officially bilingual English-French country on the continent. This is why both

names "Cameroon" and "Cameroun" are used. (This is also why I was sent to Cameroon—to teach English in a French-speaking lyceé.) In 1972 the constitution was changed and the country adopted a new name, the "United Republic of Cameroon," erasing any mention of separateness or partnership. Even the flag was symbolically changed: two stars were replaced by a single star in the center of the flag. This was the beginning of West Cameroon becoming integrated into "Cameroun," which appears to be causing tension and unrest as reported in newspaper articles, blogs, and commentaries. Since the country was "unified," the constitution has been changed again by adding another layer of government – a Senate.

The only issue that raised eyebrows was the fact that the current president, Paul Baya, is in his 80s and has been president for over 32 years! His party, the Cameroon People's Democratic Movement (CPDM) has won a sizeable majority in the legislature since he became president. It doesn't seem that there will be any change anytime in the near future. The people I spoke with accept this fact and seem to be waiting until President Baya dies for new leadership to emerge.

My visit coincided with national elections, and there were many public displays of dresses and shirts with the president's image.

What surprised me was the reaction to the former president, Ahmadou Ahidjo. The people I met spoke well of him, pointing out nostalgically that he was the country's first president, left office voluntarily, and was a catalyst for progress and change.

A political street banner

YES! A PATRIOT FOR PARLIAMENT

TIMELINE OF MODERN CAMEROON HISTORY

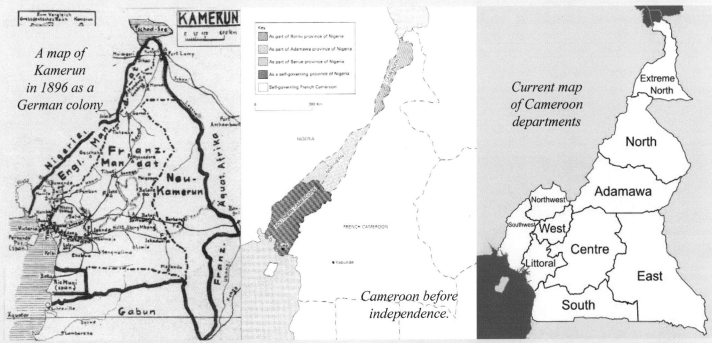

A map of Kamerun in 1896 as a German colony

Cameroon before independence.

Current map of Cameroon departments

1884 - The German Empire claimed the territory as the colony of Kamerun.

1914-1916 - During World War I, Cameroon was occupied by Allied Troops.

1919 - With the defeat of Germany in World War I, Kamerun became a League of Nations mandate territory and was split into French Cameroun and British Cameroons.

1922 - Britain and France were granted separate United Nations mandates.

1946 - The League of Nations mandates were converted into United Nations Trusteeships.

The maps are taken from government textbooks I bought while in Bafoussam: "Histoire du Cameroun" (1960) and "Cameroon History for Secondary Schools and Colleges" by V. G. Fanso (1989)

January 1, 1960 - French Cameroun gained independence from France under President Ahmadou Ahidjo.

October 1, 1961 - The British Southern Cameroons united with French Cameroun to form the Federal Republic of Cameroon.

1972 - The federal system of government was abolished in favour of a United Republic of Cameroon.

November 4, 1982 - President Ahidjo left power to his constitutional successor, Paul Biya.

52

HISTORY OF CAMEROON THROUGH STAMPS

1896 - German stamp

1906 - First stamp

1915 - During W.W.I

1916 - French occupation

1925-38 French Mandate

1953-60 British Trust Territory

1939-40 French Mandate Mandara Woman

1960 - Independent state

1960 - President Ahidjo First President

1962 - Republic of Cameroon President Ahidjo & Prime Minister Foncha

1984 - President Pul Baya

2011 - National flag

A Visit with the Prefet of Mbam-et-Inoubou

We made a courtesy call at the Préfecture or County Government Building. We walked up the stairs to the secretary's office. The building was amazingly the same as forty years ago. The Préfet, Fritz Dikosso-Sene, the highest ranking official of the county (department), arrived to

take us into an office marked 1er Adjoint (First Assistant). He obviously had no idea who we were and didn't feel we should

be allowed in his office. He was a youngish man, late forties, pompous and stiff, speaking excellent English. He looked me up and down with evident disapproval (jeans and hiking boots was not the best attire for an official visit, but it was all I had on this trip). Paul told his story about living in Bafia for two years, financing the construction of an elementary school, and teaching at the high school. Paul gave him two framed photos: one of the Préfecture and one of an Independence Day ceremony, both taken in 1970. Paul also gave him a CD with pictures of Bafia in the early 1970's, a copy of his book about his life there as a Peace Corps Volunteer, and a collection of old Cameroonian stamps. At this point the Préfet warmed up considerably and even invited his second in command to come in and meet us. He then he took us into his office (elegant mahogany furniture and the trappings of power), put on his jacket and posed for the "official" photo with his guests. He invited us to go with him to meet the new Peace Corps Volunteers.

The Préfet and his entourage sat in chairs in the front of a large hall: the Police Commissioner, the Chief of the National Police (gendarmerie), the Préfet's bodyguard, the prison warden, the Sous-Préfet (second in command). If only I could have taken a photo—suits and uniforms with lots of medals, tassels and badges. The Préfet made a speech, David (the Peace Corps representative) explained the administrative system of Cameroon, and Paul got up to speak. He started getting emotional and choked up, recovered and explained to the volunteers what a life changing experience they were embarking on. I added a few words about getting more than you give. When the meeting ended we chatted with few of the volunteers. Before leaving we visited the outdoor restrooms, complete with the bucket of water necessary to flush the toilet with. No real plumbing; just like in the old days! (Go to pge 99 for more information about our visit with the Prefet.)

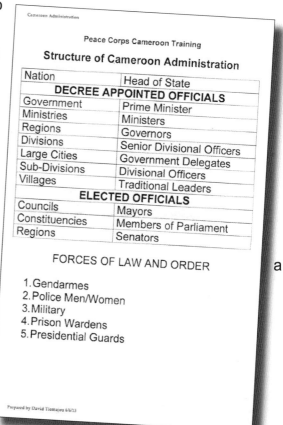

Cameroon Administration

Peace Corps Cameroon Training

Structure of Cameroon Administration

Nation	Head of State
DECREE APPOINTED OFFICIALS	
Government	Prime Minister
Ministries	Ministers
Regions	Governors
Divisions	Senior Divisional Officers
Large Cities	Government Delegates
Sub-Divisions	Divisional Officers
Villages	Traditional Leaders
ELECTED OFFICIALS	
Councils	Mayors
Constituencies	Members of Parliament
Regions	Senators

FORCES OF LAW AND ORDER

1. Gendarmes
2. Police Men/Women
3. Military
4. Prison Wardens
5. Presidential Guards

Prepared by David Tiomajou 6/6/13

53

TOURISM

Although Cameroon has many natural wonders, it is not a major tourist destination. For those who visit Cameroon, they will find that there is less infrastructure to accommodate tourism than in East Africa. Those who visit seem to be adventure-seeking individuals/couples who depend on themselves for transportation, lodging, and everything else.

Cameroon is a very diverse country both ethnically and geographically and has something for everybody. Cameroon has a long coast of beautiful pristine beaches (Limbé in the northwest and Kribi in the south), tropical rain forests and rivers (Lobé River and Falls), Mt. Cameroon (the second highest volcano in Africa), wild animal reserves (Waza in the extreme north), cheferies in the northwest (Bandjung), a sultan's palace (Foumban), and the list goes on.

During our two-week trip, we encounter only three foreign tourists: a young Frenchman at the Sultan's palace in Foumban and a South African couple at the Cheferie de Bandjung. From what information I could gather, I learned that most tourists are Cameroonians, themselves. For example, during the dry season, the more well-to-do residents of the country flood the hotels in Limbé and Kribi, two costal cities. The only large group we encountered were American medical missionary volunteers who were on their way to spend a few weeks helping out at regional hospitals.

As the infrastructure improves and the country remains politically stable, there is no reason why Cameroon can't become a major African tourist destination.

SOUVENIR DE YAOUNDÉ

Sightseeing

The Chefferie de Bandjoun & Musée de Bandjoun

Chefferie Bandjoun B.P. 141 Ouest - Cameroun
Tel: (237) 907 48 34 / 920 86 60 / 731 17 77
E-mail: museebanjoun@yahoo.fr • Site: www.museumcam.org

We stopped at the Chefferie de Bandjoun and the museum (on our way to Bafoussam). We had been there forty years ago. Unfortunately the main building had burned down eight years ago and was rebuilt but not in such a grand fashion. The wood carvings were gorgeous, but not as intricate as in the past. We started our visit (with the obligatory tour guide) at the museum, which had tools, decorative items and lots of fabulous beadwork, but the objects were badly presented and very badly lit. Then we were taken to the sacred "temple". By that time I was quite sick and kept hiding in dark corners to vomit into one of the many airplane bags that I kept in my tote. What a thing to do in a sacred place. I was so embarrassed and could hardly focus on what I was seeing. This was too bad because I had been looking forward to revisiting a place that had so impressed me in the past. *(Read more about the Chefferie de Bankjung on page 118.)*

Sultan's Palace in Foumban

After lunch we went to the Sultan's Palace, which was well-preserved. The only difference being fewer palm trees in the courtyard. We visited the museum where the rules were strict: one guide, no photos, and three visitors at a time. The museum had a stunning collection of art that was very badly presented. The lack of lighting made the Sultan's feather headdress almost impossible to see in the dark, the cases of artifacts were coated in dust, and fabulous beadwork was tucked in dark corners. The stairs leading to the different levels were extremely steep. The third person in our party was a Frenchman and I was shocked to see another tourist. He was discreet and didn't share the reason for his visit. We were told that a new building would open soon (?) to house the collection in a better setting. Considering the beauty of the objects and the interesting displays, that will be wonderful. *(Read more about the Sultan's Palace on page 139.)*

A Visit to the Mefou Ape Sanctuary

We drove to the Ape Sanctuary about 45 minutes away (from Yaoundé). ... After that very bumpy ride we arrived at the Mefou Center and were greeted by a Belgian woman who was a volunteer. We paid the 7500 CFA entry fee for us and the driver and gave her a 5000 CFA donation. She was so grateful. But she had no idea what we were going to give her at the end of our visit.

Our guide, Elvis, was very knowledgeable and took us on an extended tour. Dieudonné had never been (too expensive for him and his family) and he was thrilled. There were enclosures for the different kinds of primates: chimps, drills, baboons, gorillas. Surprisingly, at the first enclosure we met what Elvis called the escape artist sitting on a post outside the gate. He said that she went in and out as she pleased because she was sweet, bothered no one, and didn't try to run away, which would be a death sentence for her.

The chimps were hilarious. We had the lineup of three "see, hear and speak no evil" sitting there near the fence watching us. Then they followed us as we walked along the path: one kept grabbing clumps of earth and throwing them at us, another kept stopping to masturbate. Elvis said that he obviously liked me!

The baboons were feisty and the drills absolutely gorgeous, tiny with distinctive markings. We went through the forest trail, more like the jungle trail: very densely packed trees and ferns, climbing plants, some very exotic fruit. A big red fruit had an inside that resembled a litchi—mother of pearl white. Dieudonné ate one, which he said was crunchy and delicious. After this past winter's fiasco with the babaco in Ecuador, I didn't think I wanted to risk trying it. There was also wild ginger: a small red pod that didn't look like ginger but smelled like it. Elvis ate that. There were also centipedes—the edible and inedible kind. The edible ones had red hairs, but no one tasted them. Ebony trees, giant ayous trees almost as tall as sequoias, psychotria, which has fruit with psychedelic capacities---didn't try that either!

We had a few problems with the driver ants. When they crossed the path we could jump over them (still getting a few in our shoes and pants). But at one point they were all over the path so we had to run quickly through the river of ants, lifting our legs high in the air. I was carrying my usual "saddlebags' of stuff and that was not an easy feat. My brother almost lost his trousers in that mad dash. When we got to a safe place they were crawling all over us (even up to my neck). So we stomped our feet and squished them under our clothes hoping not to get too bitten. They really hurt.

Except for the ants I was thrilled with the jungle walk, so rich in color and smells, so many different kinds of trees, plants and fruit, insects and butterflies. And the humidity! I was coiffed like a poodle by the time we exited the jungle to get back on the wider dirt paths. Off to see the gorillas: huge, placid, almost Zen like in their attitude. They didn't like to be stared at and they almost dared you to look at them with their soulful eyes. They sat near the enclosure, arms akimbo, and watched. Our guide told us that if they started banging their chests and grunting it meant they were furious and it would be dangerous to be around them. Bobo was the silverback and all the females mated with him only. The younger males just had to wait their turn. It was interesting to see the different reactions of the primates: gorillas so placid but menacing, chimps so noisy and agitated, showing toothless smiles. We were told that if they showed their teeth it meant they were angry. The nursery for the orphan chimps was interesting. About twenty babies were raised together to form a group. Their mothers had been killed for bush meat or illegal pet trade and they couldn't survive in the wild. They couldn't be put in with the other chimps because the females would ignore them and the males might kill them outright. They were playing together, rolling around in the dirt climbing all over the place, playing with old tires—just like little kids. The entire sanctuary was full of rescued primates and they lived in huge enclosures in the rain forest/jungle. The gorillas and chimpanzees were being hunted to extinction and this sanctuary was important to protect them.

When we finished the tour we asked to speak to the Belgian woman, Ruth I think. We gave her the $1000 that Paul had collected in a fundraiser in West Hollywood (and that he had carried in his shoes for fear of being robbed and losing it). She was shocked by the generous donation. It would go a long way. We learned later that it would be used to buy milk to feed the baby orphan chimps for six months. We took pictures of Paul, Ruth and Elvis holding the diploma that Paul had printed up and the ten $100 bills. The people who had donated would be able to see where their money went. Dieudonné said that is was good to give it to a white person because you can't trust Cameroonians. I hated to burst his bubble but corruption knows no race or nationality. *(Read more about the Mefou Ape Santuary on page 69.)*

Lobé River and Falls

Our driver took us to the Lobé Falls, which drop directly into the ocean. We took a boat ride up the river in a (barely) modern version of the pirogue. We had a rower (pagayeur) who was personable and knowledgeable and he took us on a magical trip. We drifted, all alone, on a big, muddy river lined with baobab trees, vines, giant philodendron, bamboo, lush, dense tropical forest with not a sound except birds and the whoosh of the paddles hitting the water. We were reassured that the crocodiles were farther upstream. It was so peaceful and lovely after two weeks of what sometimes felt like chaos. Then all of a sudden on the horizon we saw two other pirogues with some Chinese men in them. It felt like a hallucination, but I remembered that the Chinese were building a deep water port about 30 km away and it appeared that the directors of the project were taking a little boat ride.

Rental boats and guides are located under the Lobé River bridge.

We went up the river and stopped to walk through the jungle where our rower pointed out various trees, vines (some that actually contain drinkable water), medicinal plants. The vegetation was dense and a little difficult to walk through. Paul had on shorts and wore no socks and was a little leery about struggling through that. I had on the jeans and hiking boots that I put on every single day and felt more comfortable. Then we were rowed back down the river: one and half hours of pure bliss. I took a picture of Paul and I—a modern version of Humphrey and Katharine in 'The African Queen", only my hat was a Panama hat from Ecuador and not Katharine Hepburn's big floppy one!

When we got back to the shore some women were washing their clothes in the muddy brown water. We had already seen some children doing the same by the beach. We climbed out of our boat, more or less gracefully, and got back into the car to drive to the beach, where we got into another boat—this time to see the falls. I had to take my hiking boots off to get into the boat and needed to take off the money purse strapped with Velcro around my ankle. Well, so much for trying to hide it! The driver and the rower both laughed.

We were rowed all along the falls and directly into them. Absolutely amazing! I had never done that before: gorgeous rocks and rushing water—and we were under it all. The falls, the beach, the sandy inlets — a real jewel of a place. (Read more on page 162.)

Lobé Falls

A newer neighborhood on the way to the airport

CONSTRUCTION

Evidence of construction is everywhere. Back then, for example, Yaoundé was a small city with one tall building in the center of town; today, there are scores of tall buildings everywhere, especially in the administrative center. Large construction sites can be seen everywhere in the country. A good example of this transformation is what is taking place in Kribi. Kribi is still an unspoiled and peaceful place, and this will soon change because of the building of a new port and a large economic zone a few miles south of Kribi. The Chinese are building a container port that will not only serve Cameroon but also adjoining countries in the Congo Basin: Gabon, Rio Muni, and the Congo. In addition, the zone includes expansive areas for mining, logging of hard wood trees, and off-shore oil drilling. The road from the new port and economic zone to Kribi is being upgraded and will probably change Kribi from being a tourist destination to a major industrial hub. The road winds along the coast and at times comes within feet of the ocean. With the widening the road, many homes and tourist hotels will have to be removed. For example, the Hotel Les Gites and its restaurant, which has just opened, will have to be destroyed to make way for the road. This is also true for other hotels along the way. With high-volume truck traffic and noise, the peacefulness of the area will be lost. Oh! The cost of progress.

FEWER EXPATRIATES

There are fewer expatriates. Years ago I saw many more expatriates; during this trip I saw a lot fewer, mostly in the Bastos neighborhood of Yaoundé where many foreign embassies and their employees live. In the 1970s the area near the Catholic cathedral along John Kennedy Boulevard was the center of town where expatriates owned stores and frequented restaurants. Today, this area is run-down with broken sidewalks, potholed streets, and crowds of street vendors. I was told that many expats left the country when the currency was devalued. Again, to use Bafia as an example, in the 1970s there were numerous expats that included members of French religious orders; European school teachers; Lebanese, Cypriot, and Greek merchants; an American doctor and his wife; and Peace Corps volunteers. During my visit, I didn't see a single white person in Bafia.

The new deep water port near Kribi.
(Photo provided by Egis Company)

BEDDING

Finally, this may seem minor, but I consider it important. When I lived in Yaoundé, I slept on a straw mattress, which was so uncomfortable that I had backaches. Today most mattresses are made of foam rubber. This has no doubt greatly improved the quality of life of the average Cameroonian. After all, we spend a third of our lives in bed.

ARRIVING IN YAOUNDE
DAY 1

We left Paris around two in the afternoon. Forty years ago I remember disembarking the airplane in Yaoundé and smelling a strange odor, which I quickly got used to. I expected to "smell" Cameroon again upon arriving when the airplane's door opened, but I didn't. This time there was no odor. Instead, I got a whiff of body odor in the plane. The collective body odor of some of the passengers was overwhelming to the point of gagging. It would be the same smell that I would encounter throughout my trip. It wasn't only body odor, but also the smell of sweaty clothing. I learned to live with it.

The flight was uneventful except for the thunder storm and lightning that we experienced when landing. It was dark outside and I could see the city lights. The plane shook and rocked from side to side which made me very uncomfortable.

We arrived at the Yaoundé Nsimalen International Airport around eight o'clock at night. The airport is small, attractive, fairly new, and far from the center of town. It serves only a handful of airlines, and is located about a half-hour's ride from the center of Yaoundé.

It didn't take very long to pass through the health department checkpoint and passport control. (I was particularly impressed by all the great-looking and colorful uniforms worn by the government employees.) Going through the health inspection was the easy part. Then we went to the baggage claim area.

When we arrived at the luggage conveyor, there was a mob of passengers who scrambled to get metal luggage carts. Any left-over carts were being hoarded by porters, and we were not able to get a cart and had to carry everything ourselves. I noticed that many pieces of luggage, packages, and boxes were wrapped in clear plastic as if someone had taken a box of some kitchen Cling Wrap® and stretched it around and around the luggage. Later, I learned that this was one way to prevent theft.

Once we got our luggage and passed luggage control, we confronted a mob of porters, taxi drivers, security personnel, and relatives waiting for passengers. It was Saturday night, and the banks were closed, and we needed to change money to take a taxi to our hotel. We were not able to buy any Cameroonian currency beforehand because it cannot be converted outside the country.

I asked a policeman (great uniform!) if he knew where we could change money, and he immediately made a quick phone call and arranged for us to meet a young woman who could change money for us on the

A view of Yaoundé from the rooftop restaurant and bar at the Tou'Ngou Hotel

spot. The woman was young, well-dressed, and very professional. She carried a small calculator and a bank bag of money. We changed 200 Euros at 620 CFA per Euro. We got 124,000 CFA. (This amount lasted us two days before we had to change money again.) The transaction took all of 5 minutes. Next, the policeman helped us find a driver. Again, he made a quick phone call, led us to the parking lot, and put us in a taxi. I gave him a 10,000 CFA tip for his help. It was well worth it. The "taxi" was an old beat-up car that could hardly handle our luggage and both of us. The driver was pleasant and talkative. He was probably a friend of the policeman and not really a taxi driver. We had a good conversation about Cameroon and he pointed out some of the interesting sites along the route. He was surprised that we already knew so much about Cameroon and Yaoundé. The taxi trip took about half an hour and cost 10,000 CFA. We arrived at our hotel about 10:30 pm.

We stayed at the Tou'Ngou Hotel, which is located at the Carrefour Etoa-Meki in the central part of Yaoundé. The hotel is made up of several buildings. The new section was in the front and our rooms were located in the old back building where the least expensive rooms are located. To get to our rooms we needed to go through a maze of hallways and staircases that I didn't really master until my third day there.

We paid $56 per day for our rooms, which were small, but clean. It even had air conditioning and a television. My only concern was that there was no toilet seat on the toilet. I immediately informed the front desk and was told that it was the weekend and they couldn't do anything about it until Monday. Later I found out that there were no toilet seats anywhere in the hotel except in Darleen's bathroom. Even that one in Darleen's room was not secured on the toilet. I managed to use the toilet with little problem and I never mentioned it again.

After getting settled into our rooms, Darleen and I went to the rooftop piano bar and restaurant for a beer. It was late and a few people were listening to the music of a singer who played an electronic piano. We finally got to bed about midnight.

The biggest predicament of the night was the loud music coming from a bar and an evangelical preacher outside of the hotel. I couldn't get to sleep until three o'clock in the morning.

I got up several times during the night to use the restroom. As soon as I switched the light on, there were scores of cockroaches running around the floor, the desk, and bathroom sink looking for a place to hide. I had to be careful not to step on them. I squirted my anti-mosquito spray around the bed and went back to sleep. During my whole time in Cameroon, I did see lots of cockroaches, but never in my bed. I learned many years ago that they are more of a nuisance than dangerous. It's part of life here.

When I walked into the bathroom, the floor was all wet. The water was coming from a broken conduit that was supposed to go from the air conditioner to the shower drain. The conduit was broken just above the door and leaked directly on the floor in front of the toilet. What do you want for $20 per night? I had to turn off the air conditioner in the middle of the night because it got too cold. Imagine being too cold in Cameroon!

A view of Yaoundé from the rooftop restaurant and bar at the Tou'Ngou Hotel

A mural on the wall of the lobby of the Tou'Ngou Hotel

TOU·NGOU HOTEL
B.P: 3626 YAOUNDE
CARREFOUETOA·MEKI
TEL: 22 20 10 25
FAX: 22 20 10 26

EXPLORING YAOUNDÉ
DAY 2

I got up at eight o'clock and was very, very tired. I'm sure that I was still dealing with a little bit of jet lag. I met Darleen for breakfast in the downstairs restaurant at nine. It's a pleasant looking place but had the most uncomfortable, rigid chairs I've ever sat in. The backs of the chairs were made of heavy, wrought iron and stood at least five feet high. We had coffee (instant coffee although Cameroon is a coffee growing country), pastries, bread, butter, jam, and an herb omelet. It was an adequate meal. The bread and pastries tasted flat because they did not have any salt.

The breakfast was included in the price of the room; however, the omelet cost extra. The servers were all young women and didn't seem to be trained. They didn't smile and stood around doing nothing. They only did what they were told to do by the manager, who had a bad habit of yelling at them in public. There was no sense of customer service that we take for granted in the United States.

Next we went to the front desk and asked if there was a hotel-recommended driver. The front desk clerk made a call. Then we met Dieu-Donné, who because our driver for the next week. We hit it off right away. He was open, talkative and knowledgeable about the

Darleen and a view of Yaoundé taken from Mont Fébé

city. He was about 40 years old, married, and had four children. His car was an older car, but it was comfortable. He said that not only would he be our driver but also would provide security. He talked a lot about "security." He made sure that all of the doors were locked and that in crowded places the car windows were not completely down. When he accompanied us away from the car, he warned of pickpockets and kept close by, always within sight.

Before the trip I bought a wallet with a chain attached to my belt. I divided my money by carrying some in my sock and some in my wallet. Darleen kept some of her money in a wallet in her bag and some in a totebag she had attached to her leg. We were always aware of our surroundings, and we never had any problems. Having Dieu-Donné around made us feel very secure.

Our driver, Dieu-Donné

The first thing we did when we got into his car was to buy a cell phone because our phones did not work in Cameroon. Dieu-Donné made a short phone call and drove us to the old commercial center of Yaoundé where we met one of his contacts. We didn't have to leave the car. We bought a new Nokia phone with an additional memory card for 15,000 CFA ($12.00!).

Dieu-Donné's car

Then, Dieu-Donné dropped us off at the Catholic Cathedral where we started our walking tour. Since we had a cell phone, we told our driver that we

would call him when we were ready to be picked up. The Cathedral is located in the area where the former Peace Corps office was located and where we used to hang out. Our first contact with average Cameroonians happened in the Cathedral. We entered the Cathedral just during the last part of a Mass. It was the part where people greet one another with a sign of peace. I had the chance to shake hands with a dozen Cameroonians, wishing them goodwill as well as being given a sign of goodwill. It was an appropriate beginning to our trip. It was a moving moment and very symbolic for me. I truly felt welcomed.

We exited through the front of the Cathedral where we saw a crowd of beggars made up of the crippled, the blind, and the elderly. It was hard walking through this gauntlet. It reminded me of the times years ago where I saw many more handicapped people. This time there were not as many. There were only a couple of times during this trip that I saw people in wheelchairs or beggars on the street.

After we left the Cathedral we walked around what was the old commercial center. It has changed dramatically for the worse. It was a shock to see how it had changed. The streets were crowded and the sidewalks were in very bad repair. There were so many people selling odds and ends on the sidewalk that we had to walk in the street. The Boulevard Kennedy used to be one of

A street scene in the old commercial center

the main thoroughfares. Today it has been reduced to just another street with dilapidated buildings. The old Peace Corps office was located on this street next to the Central Restaurant and the Artisan Center. It used to be a vibrant area where many expats would shop and hang out. Today there is an open construction pit where the Peace Corps offices used to be, the Central Restaurant is closed, and a new bank building has replaced the Artisan Center. Later I learned that most expats live, shop, and play in a new area named Bastos.

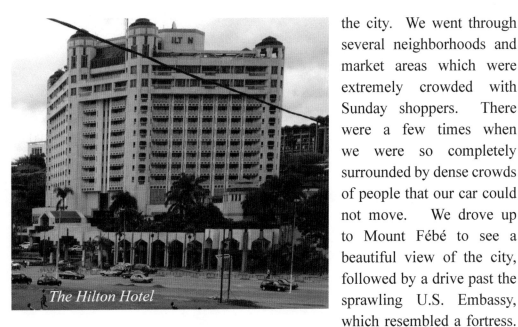

The Hilton Hotel

We walked toward the area where the old U.S. Embassy was then to the Hilton Hotel where we took a break and had a beer. The hotel sign on top of the building said "ILTN" instead of "HILTON." For me this was very symbolic of the fact that, in general, when a new structure is built, there is no or very little maintenance done to keep it in good shape. Here, it seems that things only get fixed when they are broken. When a building gets old and unusable, it is abandoned and another new building is built.

Next we called Dieu-Donné and he gave us an hour-long tour of

Paul at the Bois Sainte Anastasie Restaurant in the center of Yaounde. "33" is one of the most popular beers in the country.

the city. We went through several neighborhoods and market areas which were extremely crowded with Sunday shoppers. There were a few times when we were so completely surrounded by dense crowds of people that our car could not move. We drove up to Mount Fébé to see a beautiful view of the city, followed by a drive past the sprawling U.S. Embassy, which resembled a fortress. Next to it is the Saudi Embassy. In front of the embassy, there is a whole residential community that resembled a typical neighborhood that one would expect to see in the United States. The houses were large and well-kept with high fences and big lawns. It seems that every driveway had an expensive car on it. I even saw a white woman walking her little pet dog along the street – a sight that is only seen in the Bastos area of Yaoundé. On the way down the mountain we encountered a man selling a dead monkey – bush meat – which is discouraged but still available in all parts of the country. I guess old customs die hard.

Next we went to the Muslim part of town where we visited an artisan center to look at

crafts and artwork from Bafoussan and Foumban area of Cameroon. I bought only five wallets. There was a lot of art work. I decided to wait and come back on our last day in Cameroon when I would have an empty suitcase.

On the way back to the center of Yaoundé we passed through the Bastos area where we saw a good number of expats. There were expensive restaurants, cafés, bars, supermarkets, and all the trappings of what the central part of Yaoundé used to be like in the 1970s.

Next, our driver dropped us off at the Bois de Anastasia Restaurant in the new administrative center of town not far from the Hilton Hotel. The Bois de Anastasia Restaurant is an outdoor eatery that specializes in Cameroonian dishes. The lunch consisted of a buffet where we could sample all kinds of foods including roasted chicken, fish, and cubed beef in various sauces. There were also many cooked vegetable side dishes made with manioc, yams, potatoes, and spinach as well as several unfamiliar vegetables. A variety of cut fruit was also available, pineapple being my favorite. I sampled a little of everything. I drank beer, a "33," an old favorite. It seems that beer is drunk by everyone everywhere. It's inexpensive and has an alcohol content of about 2.5%. I am not a big beer drinker, but due to the heat I drank a lot of beer.

Checking emails at the hotel

The restaurant was surrounded by a beautiful botanical garden with a winding path and a stream going through it. To my surprise I noticed many familiar trees and plants that seemed out of place in Africa. There were eucalyptus, cypress, ficus trees, and short hedges that one might expect to see in an English or French garden. There were also a few native plants and trees. On this Sunday afternoon, the park was pleasant and being enjoyed by lots of couples and young families with children. The only distraction was the polluted stream that contained a large amount of unsightly empty bottles, plastic bags, and other trash. The water was gray and it smelled bad. What a contrast – a beautiful manicured garden with a sewer running through it.

We called Dieu-Donné with our new cell phone and had to wait an hour before he arrived. He had another client to drive somewhere. It seems that time is relative here. "It'll happen when it happens" seems to be the attitude. Some things just never change.

He picked us up and we returned to our hotel around 3 o'clock and took a nap. Around 5 o'clock I met Darleen in the hotel lobby area so we could use their Wi-Fi to read our emails and reconnect to the outside world. Wi-Fi isn't widely available in Cameroon. When it is, it is limited to a very small space – usually in the lobby area of a hotel, a coffee bar, or at cyber cafés. which we did not visit. It seemed that everybody had a cell phone, but few had a "smart" phone, tablet, or laptop computer. I met few people who used Wi-Fi while I was in Cameroon. They were mostly business people or foreigners.

We had dinner at the roof-top restaurant before going to bed. Being afraid of eating food made with sauces, we decided to stick to our rule of "cook it, peel it, or forget it." So, I had a grilled steak with French fries along with a "33" beer. The beer is made at a huge brasserie located on the way to the old airport. The factory covered acres of land and swallowed up the land and house where I lived in 1971. My old neighborhood was no longer there.

Our meal was very satisfying, and we stayed for another beer afterwards so that we could enjoy the view of the city as well as the live music.

I enjoyed the day. I felt that I didn't go through any culture shock. The culture and language were familiar, and I felt comfortable in Yaoundé. I felt that I was simply continuing where I had left off when I left Cameroon in 1972.

I wrote in my diary for about an hour and went to bed hoping that the loud music I experienced the previous night would not continue for another sleepless night. It turned out to be a fairly quiet night and I slept well – cockroaches and all.

We had breakfast as usual. While we ate I asked our waiter to ask the kitchen staff to make two ham sandwiches for our day trip to the Mefou Primate Sanctuary. We got a chance to check our emails in the front lobby before being picked up by Dieu-Donné.

Our first stop on our trip was to get gas, bottled water, and snacks for our visit. It was a shock when I entered the Total gas station mini-store. I felt that I was in the U.S. or Europe. The store was clean, had everything that one would normally see in a store in Los Angeles: sodas, bottled water, snacks, candy, small sandwiches, etc. There was even an ATM machine in the corner. I used the restroom which was clean, but like everywhere else, didn't have a toilet seat. Gas costs about the same as it does in the U.S.

The trip to the sanctuary took about 45 minutes. It is located just south of the international airport. There is a charge of 500 CFA for the use of sections of the main roads in Cameroon. When we stopped at each toll station, we were inundated by vendors selling bottled water, fruit, peanuts, and insect grubs, which are pupae of moths that live in the bark of palm trees. Five or six are placed on a thin bamboo stick and roasted. Dieu-Donné said that he hadn't eaten breakfast so he bought a few sticks. He offered us a taste, but I declined this delicacy. It looked too gross to eat.

Grilled moth pupae grubs are a delicacy

Once we left the main highway, we took a narrow dirt road for about 10 miles through a dense forest. The road went through a few villages, passed a school, and, unexpectedly, a Greek Orthodox church, and a bridge. As we got closer to the sanctuary, the road got worse, to the point that I didn't know if we would make it. Had it been raining, the road would have been impassable.

A Greek Orthodox church on the way to the Mefou Primate Santuary

We finally arrived at the main camp of the Mefou Primate Sanctuary, which consists of a small village. There is a row of small buildings where the employees live, a classroom used for children during field trips, a small reception area, a snack bar, a restroom, a picnic area with one table, an enclosure for the young chimps, and a nursery where the infant primates are taken care of.

We were greeted by Elvis Jumkarda Chefor, one of the guides. He is from West Cameroon and speaks fluent

The U.S. Embassy funded this enclosure.

English as well as French. He then introduced us to a Belgian volunteer, Ruth, who was the person in charge while Director Rachel Hogan was in Yaoundé. The cost to visit the sanctuary is 2,500 CFA per person. We didn't want Dieu-Donné to miss out on this adventure so we paid for him. We were told that the tour of the sanctuary would last several hours and that we would be hiking several miles through the forest to see all of the small primate, chimp, and gorilla enclosures. We made sure that we had enough bottled water and that we used the bathroom before starting out. I learned that on a typical day there were only one or two visitors; we only met one other group during our stay. They were members of the Air France flight crew that were on our flight from Paris to Cameroon. What a small world.

Before beginning our hike, I told Ruth that we would like to see her before we left the sanctuary because I had a surprise for her. I didn't say what the surprise was. I didn't want to give her the $1,000 donation I had with me just yet. I wanted to wait until after our visit.

We walked for about a half a mile before we reached our first enclosure. The path was rough, narrow and uneven. There was a thick canopy which didn't let much sunlight in. We had to be careful where we put our feet. As we walked, Elvis gave us a quick botany lesson by pointing out all kinds of plants, trees, fruits, and flowers. We saw cocoa trees with their colorful pods,

CARTE DU PARC NATIONAL DE LA MEFOU

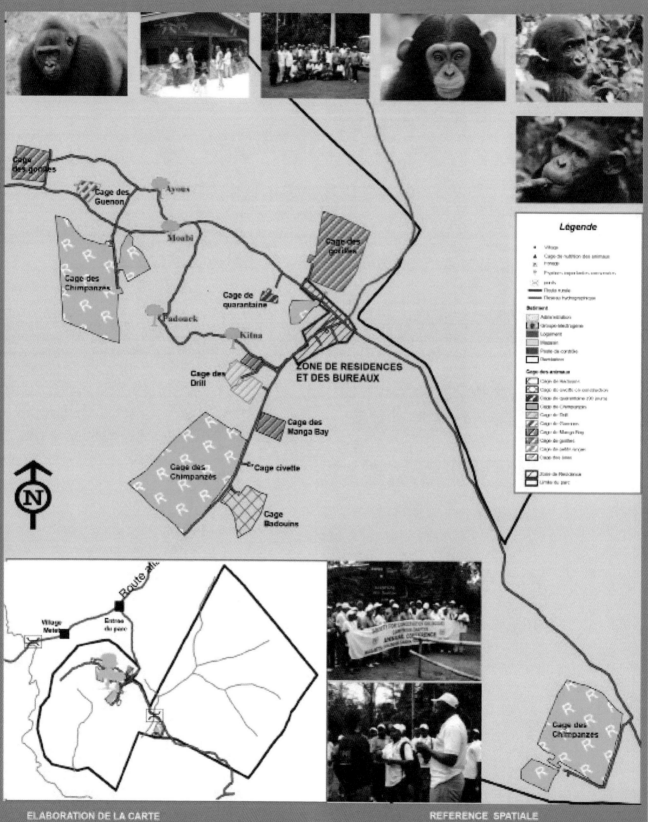

Légende

- Village
- Cage de nutrition des animaux
- Forage
- Points importants communs
- ponts
- Route rurale
- Réseau hydrographique

Bâtiment
- Administration
- Groupe électrogène
- Logement
- Magasin
- Poste de contrôle
- Plantation

Cage des animaux
- Cage de Mandarin
- Cage de civette ou contrefaite
- Cage de quarantaine 100 jours
- Cage de Chimpanzés
- Cage de Drill
- Cage de Manga Bay
- Cage de gorilles
- Cage de petit singes
- Cage des ânes
- Zone de Résidence
- Limite du parc

ELABORATION DE LA CARTE

Cette carte est réalisée par The Society for Conservation GIS Cameroon Chapter avec la participation de l'équipe de gestion du Parc National de la Mefou. Source des données: Les données existantes (limite du parc), celles provenant de la digitalisation (cours d'eau) et des travaux de terrain (infrastructures du parc) ont servi à l'élaboration de la carte.

Juin 2011

REFERENCE SPATIALE

Projection : Universal Transverse Mercator (UTM)

Datum : Clarke 1880

Echelle 1:7 387

Employee housing

Elvis Jumkarda Chefor, our guide

Environmental Education Center

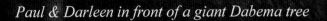
Paul & Darleen in front of a giant Dabema tree

wild ginger, and a "monkey butt" fruit, which looked like the red rear-end of a certain kind of monkey. We also saw a large spider, a long millipede, an ant nest high in a tree, and termite hills. Because the jungle was so thick we were constantly told to stay together and not get out of sight.

We came to our first chimp enclosure, which contained about two dozen members. We were told not to approach the electrified fence and to stay at least 10 yards away. The sign in front of this chimp enclosure indicated that it had been constructed using U.S. Embassy funds. This made me proud that the U.S. is helping out. At the edge of the enclosure, we were also told not to make eye contact, not eat in front of the apes, and not make any gestures. We were told to stay calm and speak softly. Elvis made a few "ooh, ooh" calls and three chimps came to investigate. Apparently, chimps are

very curious and want to check everything out. As we continued along the fence, several chimps followed us. At one point, a grey haired adult chimp came running and threw dirt at us. I was told that he was in charge and was protecting his territory. At one point Elvis told us to stand back while he took Darleen's camera and went up to one of the chimps to take some fantastic close-up photos.

The enclosure was so big that I could not see where it ended. It was as large as the size of a city neighborhood. The enclosure was surrounded by an electrified fence that used solar power, which sometimes didn't work. The day we were there it did work because we could hear the crackles of electrical shorts in the lines. The primates live off the land, but during certain times of the year when some fruit that grows naturally in the

One of the chimp enclosures
built by the U.S. Government

I AM NOT YOUR SERVANT

I am not your servant
or your slave.
I am not your research tool
or your organ farm.
My flesh is not your dinner
nor my bones your aphrodisiac.
My skin is not your luggage
or your shoes.
I am not your target or your prey
and it is not my job
to entertain you.

I am like you,
a unique expression
of the soul.
It does not matter
whether you think my life
is significant
or beautiful,
only that you know
I am significant
and beautiful
to others of my kind.

—AMBER WATSON

www.cwaf.org

enclosures is not available, it is necessary to supplement their diet with additional fruit and vegetables. On our trek through the forest we came across an employee with a wheelbarrow full of pineapples heading toward one of the enclosures.

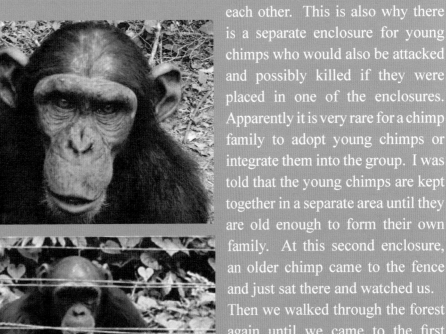

Next we passed several other smaller enclosures that housed baboons and other smaller primates. One monkey was outside of its enclosure. We didn't bother it and it didn't bother us. We moved on. It was early afternoon and many of the animals were taking a nap.

The walk to the next enclosure was more difficult. We walked on a barely visible path where we had to climb over fallen tree stumps, jump over ditches, and jump over a ribbon of black ants.

We passed by a second chimp enclosure which contained a different family. Elvis told us that families of chimps need to be separated because there is a good chance that groups would fight with each other. This is also why there is a separate enclosure for young chimps who would also be attacked and possibly killed if they were placed in one of the enclosures. Apparently it is very rare for a chimp family to adopt young chimps or integrate them into the group. I was told that the young chimps are kept together in a separate area until they are old enough to form their own family. At this second enclosure, an older chimp came to the fence and just sat there and watched us. Then we walked through the forest again until we came to the first gorilla enclosure. I had to be very careful where to walk because there were logs to climb over, lots of hanging vines to push aside, and insects to avoid--especially hanging spiders on huge webs. It was like I imagined a Tarzan movie to be like. We encountered another river of ants. The ants were a

74

A chimp family

An older chimp

Curious chimp

Young chimps enclosure

real concern because we couldn't just jump over them; we had to run across a river of them stretching about 25 yards wide. We were told to lift our feet as high as we could while running. I literately lost my pants. They almost fell down to my knees. As I was running, I had to hold them up while I was carrying my camera and my bag that was over my shoulders. After getting through the ants, we stopped and quickly picked them off ourselves and others. They bit, but not enough to cause any real problem. I got bit several times and a few climbed all the way up to my underwear. (Later that evening, I found two crushed ants in my underwear.) A bite felt like a slight prick. If I had stood in the middle of a stream of ants, it would have taken only several seconds before I would have been covered by them. I was told that we were lucky not to have encountered the more dangerous red soldier ants, which have been known to sting and kill anything in their path.

By this time I was exhausted. I was wet, sweaty, and I started getting a headache. I thought I was going to have a stroke. We

Other primates at the santuary

finally made it to the gorilla enclosure where I sat down to rest. I drank the rest of my water and had a cookie that I had brought with me. I felt better in about fifteen minutes.

The gorilla enclosure was unlike the chimp enclosure; this one had two layers of electrified fences. There are about a dozen gorillas in this family. We could see a few younger gorillas taking a nap on a covered wooden platform where they are usually fed. One of them came by to check us out, then went back to the platform. Elvis made some calling sounds and a large silverback named Bobo came right up to the fence. He just sat there calmly and watched us watching him. Unlike the chimps, which were in constant movement and climbed trees, gorillas were more laid back. We were reminded not to make eye contact or make any quick movements. After a few minutes he must have gotten bored and disappeared into the thick forest underbrush.

Again we walked along a barely discernible path on our way to the other gorilla enclosure. This one also had a family of about a dozen members. We saw glimpses of a few gorillas, but they didn't approach us.

We headed back to the base camp. On the way we passed a smaller enclosure that housed young chimps who were playing with each other. They didn't pay any attention to us and we just watched them for a while before we went to the picnic area where we ate the sandwiches we had brought with us. I had finished my water and was feeling really dehydrated. Dieu-Donné bought some more bottled water at the tiny snack bar, and I drank a whole liter bottle right on the spot.

I asked Elvis if he could go and get Ruth to meet with us before we left because we had a surprise for her. Unbeknownst to Elvis and Ruth, I had a $1,000 cash donation that I had in my sock. I also had a certificate stating the money was raised through a fund-raiser in West Hollywood. I gave her the money and had a photo taken of me presenting the money and certificate to her and Elvis. Ruth was very surprised and curious about why and how I raised the money, especially since I knew little about the sanctuary beforehand. I explained that I wanted to give

back something to Cameroon and this was my way of doing it. Ruth said that the money was enough to pay for a six-month supply of milk for the infant primates. I was especially impressed with Elvis. He was a great guide. He is young, bright, bilingual, handsome, well-educated and has a bright future ahead of him because of his experience at the park. He gave me his card and I plan on sending him photos of our trip to the sanctuary.

It was very satisfying helping out the sanctuary. I also felt relieved that I didn't have to carry around all that money. This is a special trip that few people have experienced, and I was one of them. I shall never forget it. I hope one day the average Cameroonian will be able to visit this park and see what a treasure they have in the wildlife of their country.

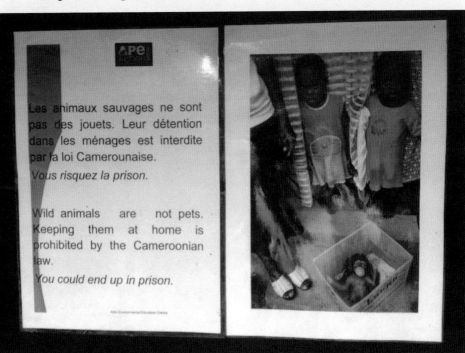

Paul presenting $1000 in cash to the Mefou Primate Sanctuary

We headed back to Yaoundé during what seemed to be rush hour. It took us about an hour to get back to the hotel where I took a quick shower and crashed until dinner. We had dinner at the hotel and went to bed early.

78

A WALK IN THE FOREST

Butterfly

Spider

Braken fern

Millipede

Our guide, Elvis, led us through the forest

Spider

Wild coco pod

Wild ginger

nt nest in a tree

Dabema tree

Ebony tree

FOREST
TRAIL

GORILLAS

Gardez notre forêt
propre.
Mettez les ordures
dans les poubelles.

Keep our forest
clean.
Please put all litter in
the bins provided.

Termite hill

Monkey butt fruit

Darleen and Dieu-Donne returning to the base camp

MORE OF YAOUNDÉ
DAY 4

BUREAU PHILATELIE
STAMP COLLECTING

After our usual hotel breakfast, Dieu-Donné picked us up, and we started out at the National Museum, which is still not open to the public. The National Museum is the old presidential palace, which sits on beautifully manicured grounds in the center of the city. It was closed, so we went on our way. As far as I know, the museum had been scheduled to open three years ago, and it still isn't ready. Pity.

Next we went to the central post office, where I tried to find the philatelic office to buy postage stamps for my collection at home. I knew there was an office for stamp collectors, but nobody seemed to know where it was. A window clerk told us to go to the back of the post office and ask there. We came across a young woman who was asleep at her desk; she didn't know anything. Then, we asked her supervisors who told us that we had to go to a smaller post office across the street from the Hôtel de Ville (City Hall). We found the philatelic office hidden behind the main building there. The office consisted of a small room, two desks, and a small display case with a few stamp albums. It was

The women who work in the Stamp Collecting Office

83

staffed by two pleasant women who were very helpful. When one of the women learned that we were going to Bafia, she seemed excited because she had been a student at the Lyceé de Bafia where I had taught. The women told us that there were not many people who came to the office to buy stamps. Most of those who did were Chinese—a big surprise to me. I stayed there for about half an hour looking through all the stamps they had. I left with newly issued stamps as well as older stamps dating from the 1980s. I spent $180 for stamps that would greatly enhance my collection. It seems that Cameroon does not issue as many stamps as they used to, maybe because of the Internet or the availability of

Entrance to the Peace Corps Offices

cell phones. Whatever the reason, modern stamps are rarely seen for sale, even on eBay, where they sell at a premium for as much as older classical stamps. Next door to the post office was the old Hotel de l'Unite where I spent many days long ago. Unfortunately, it was closed for repairs.

Next we went to the Peace Corps office, not knowing what to find. Forty years ago the Peace Corps Office was located on Boulevard Kennedy in the center of the city. Today, the old Peace Corps office building is no longer there. It has been torn down and is a construction site for a new building. The current Peace Corps office is located a little further from the center of town near the sports stadium. Forty years ago anyone

Darleen and a Peace Corps staff member in front of the my collages of photos from when I served in the Peace Corps in 1969-72

84

could just walk into the Peace Corps Office. Today it is a fortress compound with high walls, security gates, interior security guards, and Cameroonian soldiers guarding the exterior. We entered the guard house, identified ourselves, and asked to speak to the director. To our surprise we were

The former Hotel de l"Unite

CAMEROON COUNTRY DIRECTORS

LARRY WILLIAMS	1962
BILL DRETZEN	
MURRAY STEWART	
Dr ARTHUR THIE SEN	1969-1973
GRAIG KINZEI - MAN	1974
NORMAN RIFKIN	1975
JIM EKSTROM	1976-1978
ROSEMARY GEORGE	1978-1979
CONSTANCE FREEMAN	1979-1981
DAVID BELLAMA	1981-1984
KATHY CHANG DRESS	1985-1986
STEVE TAYLOR	1987-1990
STEVE LEVAKE	1990-1991
JOHN CARTER	1991-1994
MICHAEL FINLEY	1994-1995
WALT OGRODNIK	1995-1996
ROBERT HANA WALT	1996-1999
Dr JIM DOBSON	1999-2002
ROBERT STRAUSS	2002-2007
JAMES T. HAM	2007-2009
Dr LAHOMA SMITH ROMOCKI	2010-2012
JACQUELYN GEIER SESONGA	2012

immediately taken to and warmly welcomed by the country director, Jacquelyn Geier Sesonga. We visited with her for about 20 minutes and were invited to return to the office after lunch to meet a new batch of 55 volunteers who were scheduled to go to Bafia to begin their training on the following day. Coincidentally, Darleen and I would also be arriving in Bafia the following day. What serendipity!

After a very satisfying visit, we asked Dieu-Donné to take us to the best restaurant in Yaoundé for lunch. He took us to *Café de Yaoundé*. This is one of the places where "*les blancs*" (*the whites*) eat. It is owned by a very pleasant Italian man who has lived in Yaoundé for the last 15 years. He was very congenial and we spoke in Italian, a language had I learned when studying at the University of Florence in 1967.

The restaurant is set in a lush garden hidden behind tall walls. It is comfortable, has great service, serves European style food, and is very affordable. I had sliced avocado with a vinaigrette dressing, spaghetti with Bolognese sauce, and a cold beer—heavenly!

After lunch, we went back to the Peace Corps office. After going through security again, we were taken to a classroom in the Peace Corps compound where the new volunteers were attending an orientation meeting.

They were all young and reminded me of my group four decades ago. David Tiomajou, one of the training officers, introduced us and asked us to speak to the group. I spoke about my Peace Corps experience and answered questions for about 20 minutes. I told them that I would probably see them again in Bafia.

While walking down the stairs from the Peace Corps director's office, I noticed a bulletin board on which were posted a collage of photos that I had put together a few years earlier. The collage was a PDF attachment in an email I had sent the director a few months earlier. It was really nice to see them on display for all to see. My visit to the Peace Corps office was a very satisfying experience and makes me proud to be connected with such a great organization.

We went back to the hotel, and I took a nap. We had dinner again at the rooftop hotel restaurant.

That night I got sick. I had wondered how long it would take. Forty years ago I was sick almost every day from dehydration, diarrhea, malaria, stings, ticks, and you-name-it. I thought that it would only be a matter of time before I got sick on this adventure. It began with a headache, diarrhea, and the chills. I thought it might have been caused by something I ate, but I wasn't sure. I bundled up, took a tablet of Cipro, and drank at least two liters of water during the night. In the morning I felt much better. I believe it was due to dehydration. I think that the Cipro tablet I took made me sicker. From then on I made sure that I drank a lot of water and carried a bottle with me at all times.

CAFE DE YAOUNDÉ

CAFE DE YAOUNDE GARDEN

A RETURN TO BAFIA
DAY 5

After our usual breakfast, we checked out. We had arranged for Dieu-Donné to spend the next four days with us. We paid him about $60 a day which included his lodging and meals. We paid for the gas and the toll road costs.

We began our trip by going to an area around the Hilton where we changed money. It was faster and easier than going to an exchange office, where the exchange rates were lower and the paper work was time consuming. Next we went to a Total gas station, which looked just like a gas station you would find in France. We filled the tank and headed to Bafia.

The road was wonderful and the scenery familiar. It took us about two and a half hours to get to Bafia. We drove through small villages, crossed the bridge over the Sanaga and Mbam rivers, and drove through Bokito before arriving in Bafia. Once we crossed the rivers, the landscape gradually changed from a jungle-like forest to the savanna with open spaces, fields of grasses, and clumps of trees. Between Bokito and Bafia, we were stopped by a road safety inspector and asked why we

were not wearing our safety belts. We found the belts wedged under the seats. We were fined 6,000 francs ($12), told to wear our seat belts, and sent on our way. From that point on, we always wore our seatbelts.

We arrived in the city of Bafia from the west end of the city, going through the commercial center. It was unrecognizable from what it had looked like in 1969. Then it consisted of a string of stores and a gas station, not more than a few blocks long on an unpaved street. Today the commercial center is located on a mile-long paved road with hundred of shops and short roads and paths leading to small neighborhoods. We continued through the commercial center until we got to our hotel, the Hotel Rim Touristique, named after the owner, Mr. Rim.

The hotel is a newly-built and attractive building that stands out from its surroundings. It is by far one of the most attractive and inviting building in Bafia. It has fewer than a dozen rooms, a small restaurant, and an outdoor bar area with a television and upstairs lounge. The rooms were small, with a foam mattress, electric fan, and

The road to Bafia from Yaounde during the dry season in 1969.

The road to Bafia from Yaounde during the rainy season in 1969.

The road to Bafia from Yaounde 2013

running water, but not hot. Unfortunately, the water had a brown color. It was better than no water at all. One room had air-conditioning. The upstairs lounge is nicely situated for watching soccer matches in the playing field across the street. Previously, the playing field had been a small lake that has since been filled in. This area is also the location of the weekly Thursday outdoor market. It was a great place to "people watch" and a place to get a snap shot of daily life.

The day before our arrival, we called the hotel to confirm our reservations, which had been made in June. We were told that there were no rooms available because the rooms were being occupied by a delegation of election officials who were there in connection with the upcoming elections. Not knowing what to find, we decided to make the hotel our first stop hoping that we would be able to find some kind of lodging.

When we arrived, the hotel receptionist again told us that, even though we had reservations, there were no rooms available. The front desk clerk called the owner, Mr. Rim, who arrived minutes later by car. Mr. Rim

is a tall, well-dressed, proud, and imposing man who, when it was time to retire, invested in Bafia by opening a hotel. He was a joy to be around and made us feel at home. Really at home. We explained our situation and he immediately arranged for two rooms to be vacated. We got our rooms, but only after having to listen to a loud and angry reprimand by Mr. Rim to his office staff for not honoring our reservations. Apparently, the hotel is used regularly by Peace Corps staff.

While the rooms were being readied, we drove to the house where I used to live. I learned that my former landlord, Mr. Benjamin Bidias, was still alive and living in the same house. Mr. Bidias is a well-know resident of Bafia. He was once the Director of the Budget for the whole country and was well-known, not only in Bafia, but also throughout the country. I knew where the house was in general, but it was difficult to find because of all the new construction that had taken place over the years. Once we got to the general area, we asked neighbors for directions and found the house with little problem.

HOTEL RIM TOURISTIQUE

Mr. Rim, the owner of the hotel

My heart beat when I saw the house. The house, made up of three apartments, has been kept in good shape and was surrounded with concrete walls with a large metal gate. It had changed very little. Behind the house there was a large yard in the middle of a small cocoa plantation. We were met by a current tenant who informed us that Mr. Bidias lived on the other side of the compound

Darleen Guien, Benjamin Bidias, Paul Hamel, Chantal Londji Dang, and Jeannette Dan a Bidias

with his wife, Jeannette Dan a Bidias. We then met Chantal Londji Dang, Mr. Bidias's niece, who took us to him. He was sitting under a thatched-roof gazebo. Darleen and I were warmly received. We introduced ourselves and, to my surprise, he remembered us. I felt that in a strange way that I had come home again. We spent about two hours talking, drinking, reminiscing about the past, and talking about his adventures in the

United States. Mr. Bidias had been all over the United States studying finance and officially representing his country. He is now 75 years old and has retired to his home town. Serendipity had followed us throughout our trip, and this was yet one more example. He gave me a good sense of how Bafia has changed, and he was helpful in giving us information and contacts that would help us during our stay. For example, Darleen and I brought a 50-pound suitcase full of dolls and teddies (donated by *"Dollys Making a Difference,"* a charitable organization based in Los Angeles), toys, school supplies, and handmade dresses (from a sewing club in Santa Barbara) to give to the most needy children we could find – perhaps an orphanage. Our main concern was that the donations go to the truly needy and not end up being sold for

Soccer players practicing in front of the Hotel Rim Touristique

92

Our newly-built home in 1969

Our home in 1971

The same house in 2013

profit. We were directed to the Préfet and the Catholic bishop.

Again, serendipity called – we got to know Chantal better. She was born in Bafia and spent her childhood in Donenkeng (an American Presbyterian Mission Hospital where I had spent a lot of time) with her mother who worked with Dr. Sandilands (a close friend of mine), who had been the American doctor there. She also attended the Lyceé de Bafia where I had been an instructor in the 1970s -- ten years before she attended. Chantal immigrated to Canada and now lives in Edmonton, Alberta. She was back in Bafia due to the death of her mother. She works at the University of Alberta as a producer of a French-language radio

The sight of small herds of Zebu grazing around Bafia is very common. This photo was taken from the Hotel Rim Touristique.

*A view of the former lake in the
administrative center of Bafia in 1969*

*The same view taken from the same spot in front
of the Hotel Rim Touristique in 2013*

station CJSR. Darleen and I hit it off immediately with her. We made arrangements to meet her the following day to accompany us to the Catholic mission in Gondon, a mostly residential and newer area of the city, to find someone who could help us distribute the donations.

After a very eventful day, Dieu-Donné drove us back to the hotel. We paid him for the day and gave him extra money for lodging and dinner. We settled into the hotel and freshened up.

Just before dusk we took a walk on the main road to the commercial center passing by the Hotel de Ville (City Hall) and watched part of a soccer game that was being played on the large grassy area in front of the building. I remembered this area as a small lake. The lake has been filled in and is now a soccer field as well as the location of the weekly Thursday outdoor market.

We strolled into the commercial center and passed a large new mosque with tall minarets. This was a different side of Bafia that I didn't expect to see. This area is heavily Christian with an apparently growing Muslim community. On our walk I looked for familiar

THEN & NOW

The road to the commercial center in 1969

The commercial center in 1971

The road to the commercial center in 2013

The commercial center in 1969

The commercial center in 2013

landmarks but was unable to identify any building I knew. When I lived in Bafia, the commercial center was dominated by a few white families from Lebanon, Cyprus and Greece. They ran a fish store, a general (and hardware) store, and a bakery. I was told that they had left long ago. The buildings they occupied were no longer there, or unrecognizable. We made it half way through the commercial center and turned around so that we could arrive back at the hotel before dark.

That night we ate dinner at the hotel. Earlier in the day I asked about a special local food called "safou," a purple fruit with a large nut that resembles a small avocado.

Roasted safou and bread

I remember eating it years ago, and I craved to experience it again. The cook made an extra effort to go to the market to get some for us.

The surface of the safou was cut in slits, and the whole fruit was roasted. We cut open the fruit, scooped out the thin layer of green pulp, and spread it on bread. It is difficult to describe the taste. Its texture is smooth and something like a cooked avocado, but the taste has a lime quality. We were careful not to eat too many not, knowing how it would affect us. Then, for our main course, we had grilled chicken, plantains, and beer. The meal was simple and filling. After eating, we went directly to bed.

The main mosque in Bafia

EXPLORING BAFIA
DAY 6

I had a quiet night. The only problem was not having a comfortable pillow. It was a bundle of irregular shaped pieces of foam. I dreaded the thought of taking a shower because there was no hot water – only cold brown water. I gritted my teeth and took the quickest shower I've ever taken. Then, I met Darleen for a breakfast of coffee, bread, and a simple omelet made with vegetables and sardines.

Our first stop was to make a courtesy visit to the Préfet, who is the chief administrative officer of the

99

The Prefecture in 1969 and in 2013

Department of Mbam and Inoubou. We didn't know what to expect. We drove to the old Prefecture building, which had been built by the French in the early days of Bafia. It's an impressive building that stands out in the administrative center of town.

While still in the United States, I printed out two large, colored, glossy photos of the Prefecture building taken during the Independence Day celebration in 1970. I had planned to present the photos as well as a small stamp collection as a present to the Préfet.

We entered the building and asked to see the Préfet. We were immediately shown to the office of the Sous-Préfet (second in command) and told to wait. A short while later, Préfet Fritz Dikosso-Seme, walked into the

Darleen, Paul and Préfet Fritz Dikosso-Seme

room and greeted us. The position of préfet commands respect so we were very formal. He spoke both French and English, and we carried on the conversation in French which was more comfortable for him. We chatted for about fifteen minutes then we went to his regular office where I presented him with the photos, a CD of old photos of Bafia, and the stamp collection. He was visibly pleased and promised to display the photos in his office. Then we had our photos taken with him. Before leaving, I told him that I had another present for him. I asked his permission to photograph some of the major sites in the city. I promised him that I would use the photos to put Bafia "on the map" -- meaning that I would post photos of all the important sites in Bafia on Google Earth. This

THEN & NOW

Independence Square in 1970 (left) and in 2013

way people who search for Bafia would be able to view the photos. He was pleased and encouraged me to do so. *(This project is yet to be completed.)*

Coincidently, David Tiomajou, the director of training for the Peace Corps, whom we had met the day before in Yaoundé, arrived at the Prefecture while we were there. David was there to accompany the Préfet to an orientation meeting for the fifty-five new Peace Corps trainees who had arrived earlier that day to begin their two month training period before being sent to towns and villages throughout the country. The Préfet asked us to accompany him to the meeting. We followed him and his motorcade of government officials: Sous-Préfet, police chief, fire chief, budget director, as well as a dozen others.

Before the Préfet spoke, we sat in on a short lecture about the political structure of the government and city services. Then, one by one, the trainees stood up and introduced themselves by stating their names, where they were from, and what kind of work they would be doing in Cameroon.

Next the Préfet welcomed them and spoke about safety and security. He introduced

Peace Corps trainees on their first day

The Catholic Cathedral of Bafia

Sister Patanebi looking at a donated dress

101

his staff and other city officials and explained their duties. He then answered questions from the trainees. Finally, the Préfet asked me to say a few words. While speaking I was overcome by emotion. I teared up at one point while referring to Bafia as "home" because the early formative years of my youth were spent there. This is a place where I learned many life skills and important lessons.

Then, we went to pick up Chantal so that she could help us find a place where we could donate our toys, dolls, teddies, and dresses. We drove to the Catholic mission at Gondon, a neighborhood of Bafia. We found the pre-school and spoke to Sister Patanebi, who had just arrived to start her new assignment as school director. Since she was not familiar with the area, she directed us to see one of the priests, who sent us to the mother superior.

We drove to a nearby convent and met a group of Ursuline nuns who educate the children in the mission schools. We wanted to know if they knew of any orphanage in the area where we could donate what we brought. They couldn't name any place. We were disappointed that we couldn't find really needy kids. So Darleen and I decided to give our donations to the children in the pre-school. There was one problem. These children did not come from poor families. In fact, these were the kids of well-to-do families who could afford to pay school tuition.

They suggested that we go back to see Sister Patanebi and work something out with her. We did so, but it was too late. So, we made an appointment to see her at 8 o'clock the following morning.

The Catholic mission of Gondon is a very impressive place in a growing neighborhood of middle class families. The mission is comprised of a large compound that includes a cathedral, rectory, library, community center, youth center, maintenance yard, schools, and other buildings that support the mission's work. Every building I saw was in excellent condition, in good repair, and freshly painted. The grounds are well-kept. This neighborhood is also where the Peace Corps training center is located and where many trainees are housed with host families.

Dieu-Donné drove us to the hotel and we asked Mr. Rim about the local restaurants and he told us to go to the Yaya restaurant for lunch. Dieu-Donné took us to the restaurant in the middle of the commercial center. It was hard to find. Darleen and I were the only ones there for lunch. There was no menu. The only food they had was grilled chicken, plantains, bread, and of course, piment sauce. The food was okay and tasted better with a beer.

Simon and Anasthasie Nwaga Nwaga with Mayra Zuniga, a Peace Corps trainee, holding their child

The Yaya Restaurant

A meal at the Yaya Restaurant

Then we picked up Chantal and went to see her uncle and aunt, Anasthasie and Simon Nwaga Nwaga, the brother of Mr. Bidias. They also live in the Gondon neighborhood. Coincidentally again, they were hosting a Peace Corps trainee, Mayra Zuniga from Northern California. Simon is a very jovial person who was excited about having us at his home. He has a bubbly personality and laughs easily. He made me feel as if I were visiting a long lost relative. We visited for about an hour and covered a myriad of subjects: his teaching experience, his education in Switzerland, the history of Bafia and the United States, politics, and the Peace Corps. In the middle of our visit, Mayra Zuniga arrived home from her first day of training. It was a big day for all of us.

We got back to the hotel about 5 pm to find out that there was no electricity. Apparently, it goes out fairly often so the hotel had to use its electric generator. It seemed like times gone by. While we waited for the electricity to come back on, Darleen and I went to the second floor outside patio to people watch. This is a great place to view a soccer game and the goings-on at the weekly Thursday outdoor market. We could also hear the rumbling and lightning of an oncoming storm.

We were not that hungry so we snacked on cookies and beef jerky that I had brought with me for just such an occasion. Of course, we had a beer, too. I hoped that it would rain that night to give us a little relief from the heat, and it did.

The weekly outdoor market in 1969

103

The weekly outdoor market in 2013

GETTING REACQUAINTED
DAY 7

The road to Donenkeng

While we were having breakfast, Dieu-Donné was already waiting for us. Our first stop was Donenkeng which is located about four miles away on a dirt road through thick forest. It is so near, but so unlike Bafia, which is more savanna. Donenkeng is a village known for its Presbyterian mission hospital and school. The mission was built around 1935 and was originally called the American Presbyterian Mission. Today the mission consists of a large church and a medical campus. The former mission school, Anderson School, is no longer operating. The land and the school buildings have been sold to the government and turned into a public lycée.

Darleen and Dr. MiLobért Mbengang, the head doctor, in front of the mission hospital

Our first stop was to see the pastor, but he was not available. So we went to find the Sandilands former home. I knew exactly where to find it. It was a short distance away along a road overgrown with weeds. I recognized the house immediately and it was a very sad and depressing sight. Once it was an "American" oasis in the middle of Africa. Today the house is abandoned and slowly being devoured by the forest. I have very fond memories of spending time there to experience a little bit of home away from home. The house used to look like a typical home one would see in the United States with awnings, flowers, and a lawn. This is where I could go to eat jelly beans and chocolate chip cookies. This was also the place

The home of Dr. Sandilands, the head doctor at the mission hospital of Donenkeng in 1969

The same house in 2013

THEN & NOW

Students of the Lycee de Donenkeng

where I had recovered from a minor operation and malaria. We spent a few minutes and left with a heavy heart.

Next, we went to find the school building that I had helped built at the Anderson School in 1971. It consisted of two classrooms, a small office and a library. I had raised $1,200 to construct the school: one thousand dollars from the American School Partnership Program and two hundred dollars from the students at Thomas Moore College in Covington, Kentucky, where my aunt was an instructor. The money was used to buy the materials, and the labor was donated by volunteers from the mission.

106

The school director in front of a lycée building

I did the architectural drawing, arranged for permits from the city, and chose the name "Martin Luther King Jr. Building." It took about four months to build. Opening day was one of the proudest days of my life. I had a general idea where the school was, but not exactly, so we went to the mission hospital office to get directions. We met Dr. MiLobért Mbengang, the head doctor of the mission. (He told us that Dr. Sandilands granddaughter had been there three months earlier to visit. Before the trip I tried to contact the Sandilands' sons, who I believe live in Oregon, but I was not successful.) Dr. Mbengang

The school I helped build in 1971

The same building in 2013

took us to the school building, which was no longer in use. We walked for a few minutes along a narrow path until we arrived at the school compound. We found the building. It was barely visible behind tall bushes and weeds. My heart sank again. We positively identified the building by looking at a photo I had taken on the day it was dedicated. It looks as if it has been abandoned for a long time, and it no longer has a roof. I walked through the building and noticed a lot of graffiti, but the walls and floor were still in good condition. If it had a new roof, a resurfaced chalkboard, and some paint, it could be used again. The good news was that there were three newer classroom buildings next to it. We met the director of the school, but he couldn't tell us very much about the recent history of the school because he had just been assigned there. I showed him the photo of the building in 1971 and gave it to him. The former Anderson Elementary School is now a government-run lyceé that serves about 150 students. The classrooms are extremely crowded with five students occupying a desk designed to accommodate only two or three students. Each classroom contains a chalkboard and little else. The classrooms have concrete floors and an aluminum roof. The windows are nothing more than square holes in the wall. Some windows have a few screens or wooden slats. This is the way I remembered my own classrooms at the Lyceé de Bafia forty years earlier. We stayed about 15 minutes and went back to the mission hospital. Darleen and Dr. Mbengang stayed at the mission; Dieu-Donné and I went back to the school with some school supplies that I had brought with me: pens, pencils, stickers, erasers, and toothbrushes. Yes, toothbrushes because a friend in California asked me to promise to buy toothbrushes with the money he donated. So, I did. I got the opportunity to visit two classes while there. I spoke to the students about my experience and answered questions. One student suggested that I find someone in the United States to donate the money to renovate the abandoned building. I told him that I would look into it. On the path on my way back to the mission, I wasn't very careful and stepped into a ribbon of ants just like the ones we encountered at the Mefou Santuary. Only a few managed to climb onto my pants, and I quickly picked them off before they had a chance to bite.

Next, Dr. Mbengang went with us to the local public elementary school where there was also a pre-school. We drove to another part of the village into a small valley where the school is located. We met with the director and visited the pre-school classroom. The classroom was decorated with paper banners and very little else. There were no toys or any other school items visible. The children looked great and extremely cute. They were between three and five years old. They all wore uniforms, were clean, and appeared well-fed -- unlike some malnourished children I remembered years ago with bloated stomachs. It was reassuring to see that there has been a lot of progress in education over the years. We gave half of the dolls and toys to the teacher and teacher's aide to keep at the school, and not to be taken home. Unfortunately, the teacher told us that she had to take all the school supplies and play things home each night because the classroom is constantly being broken into during the night. She reassured us that the dolls and teddies would be used in the classroom and she would take them home every night so they would not be stolen. Before we left, we had photos taken of the children with some of the dolls and teddies so that we could share them with those who made the dolls back in the United States. We drove back to the hospital where we finally met the pastor. He accompanied us on a tour of the mission hospital, which appeared to be stuck in time. Nothing had changed. We were told that the mission was slowly dying. Donations from the Presbyterian Church in the U.S. were slowly drying up and there was no other way to raise money to keep the hospital going. We were also told that there was no dynamic leadership since the Sandilands left. Old mission buildings remain, and there is no evidence of new construction except for the government-run schools. The pastor said that the Sandilands would cry if they were alive today. He said that all of their work died with them. I left Donenkeng disappointed with a heavy heart. I fear for Donenkeng's future. Next we drove back to the Catholic mission at Gondon, which looks like paradise compared to Donenkeng. We went directly to the pre-school where we met with Sister Patanebi. The pre-school serves the same age group as the school in Donenkeng, but these students

110

Pre-schoolers at the Catholic mission in Bafia

come from the middle-class parents who can pay high monthly tuition, which amounts to about $70 per month. Unlike Donenkeng, the classrooms had toys, books, and other school supplies. But the toys were old and there were not enough of them for the children. Before giving the donations to the school, Sister Patanegi took us to see Bishop Bala whose parish includes the whole central region of the country. Bishop Bala is very warm, gracious and inviting. He is tall and slender and appears to be in his fifties. I expected to see him wear a red cassock, bkut he wore an embroidered blue robe resembling what Muslim men wear in the north of the country. He lives in an impressive residence and his office was very imposing with all the trappings of his position. He even has a personal secretary. We met with him for about half an hour and spoke about a variety of topics: the history of the mission, his duties, and his personal story. Before leaving, we had photos taken with him. It was a very pleasant and informative meeting. Later on in the week, I got an email from Bishop Bala thanking us for our visit and our donation. Next, we went back to the pre-school where we visited two classes. As we entered the courtyard

Above Sister Patanegi, Bishop Bala, and Darleen
Below: The chief of Bafia

of the pre-school, we were welcomed by a group of children. They gathered around me, took my hand and asked me if I was Santa Claus (Pere Noel). Being 67 years old, a bit rotund, with grey hair, and bringing gifts, I could understand why they thought I was Santa. I was totally taken off guard, and I didn't say that I wasn't Santa. We gave half of our donations to the teachers who would make them available for classroom use. We had photos taken of the children with some of the dolls and teddies. Finally, we went back to Sister Patanegi's office where we visited for a while and devised a plan to save the dresses until Christmas when they would be distributed to the neediest children in the school. I had another donation that we were careful not to talk about—namely a large bag of condoms that was donated by WeHo Life, a program funded by the City of West Hollywood. I had no idea how we would distribute them, hoping that we would eventually find someone who could help us. Again, serendipity called. It turned out that our new friend, Chantal, is an activist in AIDS prevention both in Canada and in Cameroon. We told her about the condoms and she agreed to give them to a local clinic. Relieved, Darleen and I felt satisfied

Above: Lycée de Bafia in 1969

Below: The same school in 2013

Le Lycée Bilingue de Bafia
dit non à la **CORRUPTION!**
non à la **VIOLENCE!**
non à la **DROGUE!**

113

Lyeeé Classique de Bafia in 2013

Independence Square in the center of the administrative center of Bafia

with where all of the donations went. Our "mission" was over. We could now concentrate on being tourists. Darleen and I were having a bit of intestinal problems probably from the food we had over the previous few days, so we decided to go to a store where we could buy packaged food and canned goods. We found a store in the commercial center where we bought canned tuna fish, Laughing Cow cheese, butter, yogurt, jam, a baguette of bread, a chocolate bar, orange soda, and bottled water. We went back to the hotel and had a picnic on the second story terrace overlooking a herd of grazing zebu. After lunch, Dieu-Donné drove us around town to take photos of as many landmarks as we could. These photos are being used to post on Google Earth. We took photos of the prefecture building, post office, hospital, central square, schools, etc. As we were leaving the hotel, I met the Chief of Bafia who had been meeting with some of his friends at the hotel. He was accompanied by his bodyguard and wore a long blue robe and wearing a large traditional necklace made of what looked like boar's tusks. I introduced

myself and we spoke for a few minutes. One of his companions noted that he was a student at the same time I was an instructor at the Lyceé. Unfortunately, I didn't remember him. I asked to take the Chief's photo. He posed for me with a big pipe in his mouth. I thanked him, and Darleen and I went on our way. We got back to the hotel at 3:30 pm and took a nap. Around sunset, Darleen and I went back to the upstairs terrace where we had a beer, peanuts, Oreo cookies, and trail mix that I had brought from the U.S. We spent the rest of the evening planning our trip to Bafoussam and West Cameroon. Fortunately, the electricity had been turned on again. During the night it began to rain hard. The temperature dropped, and I turned off the fan in my room. I lay there and fell asleep listening to the rain on the aluminum room just as I used to do years ago. Our stay in Bafia was coming to a close and far exceeded my expectations. Our whole visit was full of good luck, coincidences, and serendipity.

BAFIA DANCERS

The traditional dancers of Bafia are well-known for their lively and exciting movements that express joy through posture and facial expressions. They have performed throughout the country and are celebrated by larger-than-life sculptures in central plaza, Independence Square. Below is a photo of the dancers taken in front of the Prefecture during the 1970 independence celebration.

VIEWS OF BAFIA

The Government Guest House

The old court house

The current court house

The community meeting hall

The post office

VIEWS OF BAFIA

Billboard and electric lines in the commercial center

The Lycée Classique de Bafia

The parade ground

The Ministry of Finance building

The Ministry of Youth building

The hospital grounds

A residence in the administrative section

A residence next to the Hotel Rim Touristique

A VISIT TO BANDJUNG
DAY 8

The day didn't start out well. When I met Darleen for breakfast, I found out that she had been sick all night.

We left Bafia about 9 o'clock. Our plan was to visit the Cheferie of Bandjung on our way north to Bafoussam.

We had visited the Cheferie in 1971 and wanted to see how it had changed. It was a pleasant ride on good roads. We drove through the savanna gradually climbing in altitude through beautiful hills and valleys where we could see hillside farms and villages. The scenery was picturesque especially with patches of blue sky and large puffy clouds. The temperature became cooler and less oppressive. It was a welcome

Cheferie of Bandjung's main meeting hall

change from the heat we experienced in central Cameroon.

We got to the Cheferie about noon. The site has somewhat changed since we last saw it. The main building had burned down and was rebuilt in the likeness of the original. The structure was built of wood logs. The roof was a traditional thatched roof, and the walls were made of woven bamboo strips. The outside of the building was surrounded by artfully carved tribal-related images.

Other buildings in the compound had also been rebuilt. The traditional roof construction of this area is tall, narrow, and pointed. Instead of conventional thatched roofs, new construction incorporates aluminum, which is inexpensive and easily available due to the large aluminum plant powered by the electricity generated by a large dam on the Sanaga River in Edea.

We took a guided tour of the museum, which was very informative. There were many objects that told the history of how iron was used to make everyday tools and ceremonial decorative art pieces. Among some

Statue of King Kamga at the entrance to the compound

The royal residence

Our tour guide

of the most impressive items were the beadwork that is used to cover baskets, clothing, statues, and thrones.

Darleen became more and more ill as the day progressed so we decided to get to the hotel in Bafoussam as soon as possible. It took us about an hour to get to our hotel.

We arrived in Bafoussam in the early afternoon and went directly to the Hotel Talotel. The city is not very attractive and is spread out with many neighborhoods covering numerous hills. Nothing stood out; every building seemed to be like the next. The roads were crowded and in very bad condition. Potholes and ruts were everywhere.

The hotel is located in the center of the city and is made up of several buildings. The hotel includes an indoor and outdoor restaurant, nightclub, bar, swimming pool, and meeting rooms. Wi-Fi was available only in a small lobby consisting of a tiny area in front of the check-in desk that had two chairs. The Wi-Fi, which was also located in the bar area, didn't work the whole time we were there.

THEN & NOW

The entrance to the Cheferie of Bandjung in 1971 (above) and in 2013 (below)

THEN & NOW

Cheferie of Bandjung in 1971 (above and bottom left.)
The Cheferie in 2013 (bottom right)

121

The entrance of the meeting hall in 1971 (left) and in 2013 (right)

BAMOUN WOOD CARVING

123

BANJOUNG MUSEUM

124

BEADED ARTWORK

BEADED ARTWORK

BEADED ARTWORK

We had decided before our trip that we would splurge a little and go to an "upscale" hotel midway through our trip. The Hotel Talotel was the best hotel we could find. We paid $100 per room per night. Apparently my definition of "upscale" means something different here. For this amount of money I expected more. The hotel was just okay. The hotel amenities were on the par with an inexpensive hotel one would find in the U.S. The rooms and the bathrooms were relatively large and clean. And, there was hot water, too. There was a king-sized bed, flat-screen TV, air-conditioning, and even a phone.

Darleen went to her room and straight to bed, and I went to the restaurant to have some lunch. Breakfast and lunch at the hotel consist of a buffet that I did not find appetizing. There was tripe, small fishes in some kind of sauce, left-over pieces of chicken, rice, and other unrecognizable food items all cooked in sauces. Nothing was hot; everything was warm and presented in large metal pans. Keeping in mind that Darleen was probably suffering from something she ate in Bafia, I decided not to have any of the food. The sauces scared me. After speaking to the servers, I was able to order a special meal from the kitchen. I ordered my old stand-by: grilled steak with French fries. The meal was good and satisfying. I washed it down with a beer. I checked up on Darleen and went to my room for a nap. During my nap, there were loud screams

A sign outside of the hotel listing the available services

Local artists are famous for their wood carving reliefs that decorate every door and piece of furniture in the hotel.

coming from teenagers in the nearby pool. Then, there were the noisy next door neighbors who had been drinking.

The sound of a text message on my iPhone woke me. I hadn't expected it to work. It was an alert that I was being charged for roaming charges. The text indicating that I had already used $300 worth and that my account would be blocked. Apparently I had not turned off the data connection function on my phone although I had put the phone on Airplane mode. I turned the data connection function off and never used it again. (When I got home, AT&T was very accommodating by dropping the charges.)

I started watching CNN on TV. For a moment I almost forgot I was in Cameroon. I got caught up on what was happening in the world. The story of the day was the terrorist takeover of a shopping mall in Kenya on the other side of the continent. We watched it play out on TV during our three days there. There are about a dozen or so TV channels that we could watch: CNN; three or four French language Cameroonian stations that carried sports, news, discussion programs, religion, and music videos; an English language station; a bilingual station; a European French language News station; and an African news station based in Gabon.

Little by little, minor inconveniences started to bother me. First, the picture on the TV kept fading out and finally gave out completely. I decided to take

a shower, but there were no towels in the bathroom. There was no Wi-Fi in the rooms and the Wi-Fi in the bar area wasn't working. These "little things" started to grate on my nerves.

I called the front desk several times to report the TV and get towels, but nothing happened. Finally, I went to the front desk and was able to get some towels. Later in the day, a hotel employee came to look at the TV and said that there was nothing he could do. He just shrugged and left. I asked the front desk staff about the Wi-Fi connection in the bar and restaurant, but they were unaware that it was not working. I asked the bartender about it, and he said that it hadn't been working for some time.

Customer service was minimal at best. Service employees stayed out of sight and never interacted with hotel guests unless spoken to. It seemed that employees were not knowledgeable about the workings of the hotel or what other employees' duties were. The longer I stayed at the hotel, the more frustrated I became. The service was not at the level it should have been for the amount of money we were paying.

The exterior of the hotel

Outdoor restaurant and bar patio

The swimming pool

The bar entrance

A typical bedroom

Before checking up on Darleen, I went to the front desk of the hotel, which was across the street. The lobby was a tiny area consisting of a reception desk and two armchairs for guests. This was the only place that Wi-Fi was available. I was able to download 75 emails, which lifted my spirits, especially after four days of isolation.

It was about 5 o'clock , so I went to check up on Darleen. She was finally feeling better, but not enough to have a big meal. We decided to go to the hotel bar area where we ordered some French fries and a beer. On the second day we had cocktails, which cost about $10 each. After a few drinks, we went back to drinking beer and eating peanuts.

During our whole stay at the hotel, the bar area was completely empty of any guests. There wasn't a single other person who came to the bar or restaurant in the later afternoon and early evening. We had the whole place to ourselves. We had comfortable chairs, beer, peanuts, our own bartender, and a TV on which we could watch anything we wanted. It was definitely relaxing, but we had hoped to meet some of the other guests and socialize. It never happened.

The bar area

The bar lounge area

A modern bathroom

The front desk

A modern shower

130

VIEWS OF THE TALOTEL

BAFOUSSAM STREET SCENES

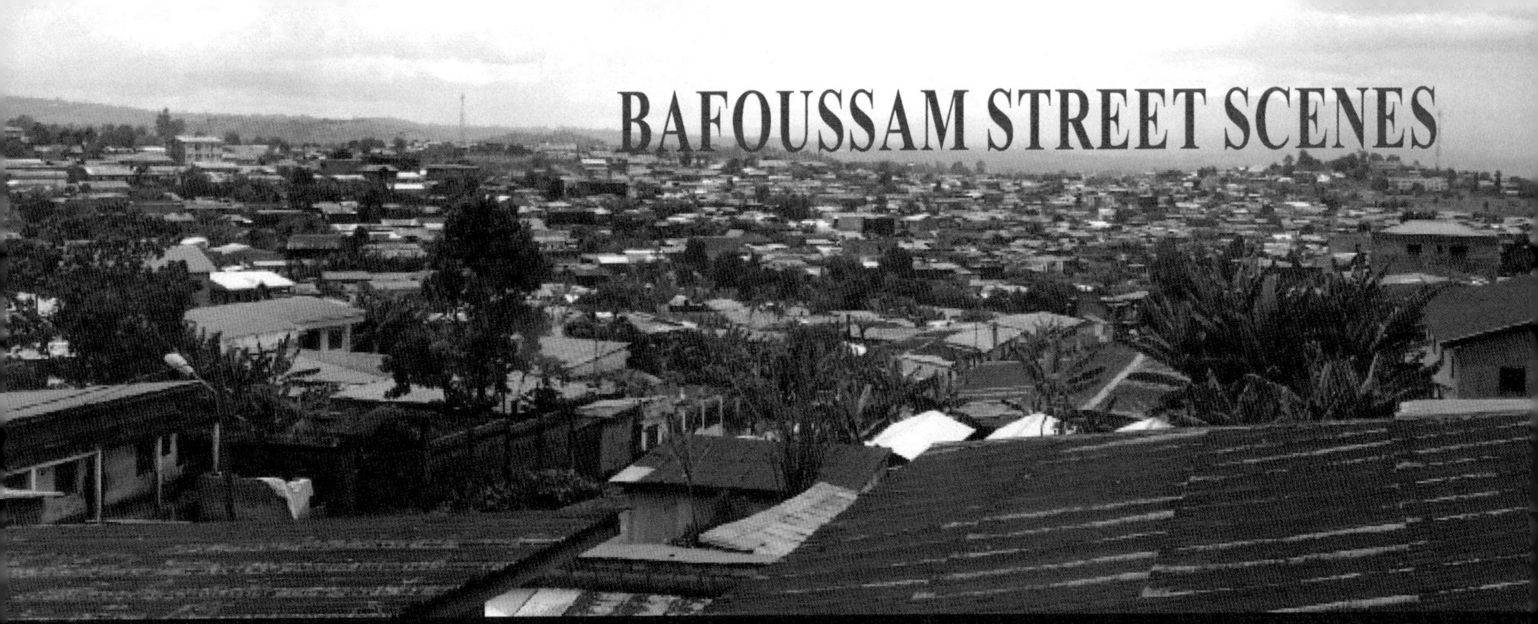

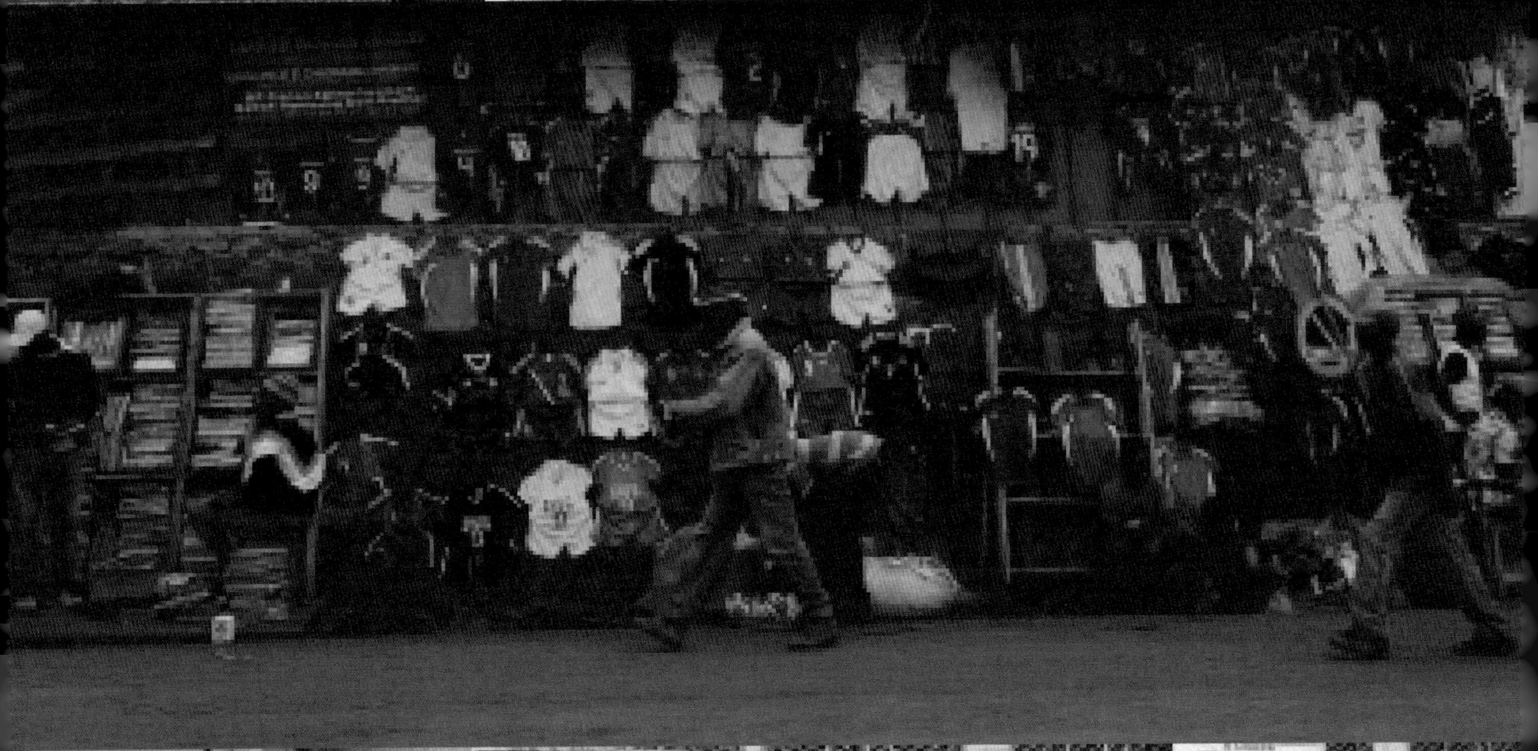

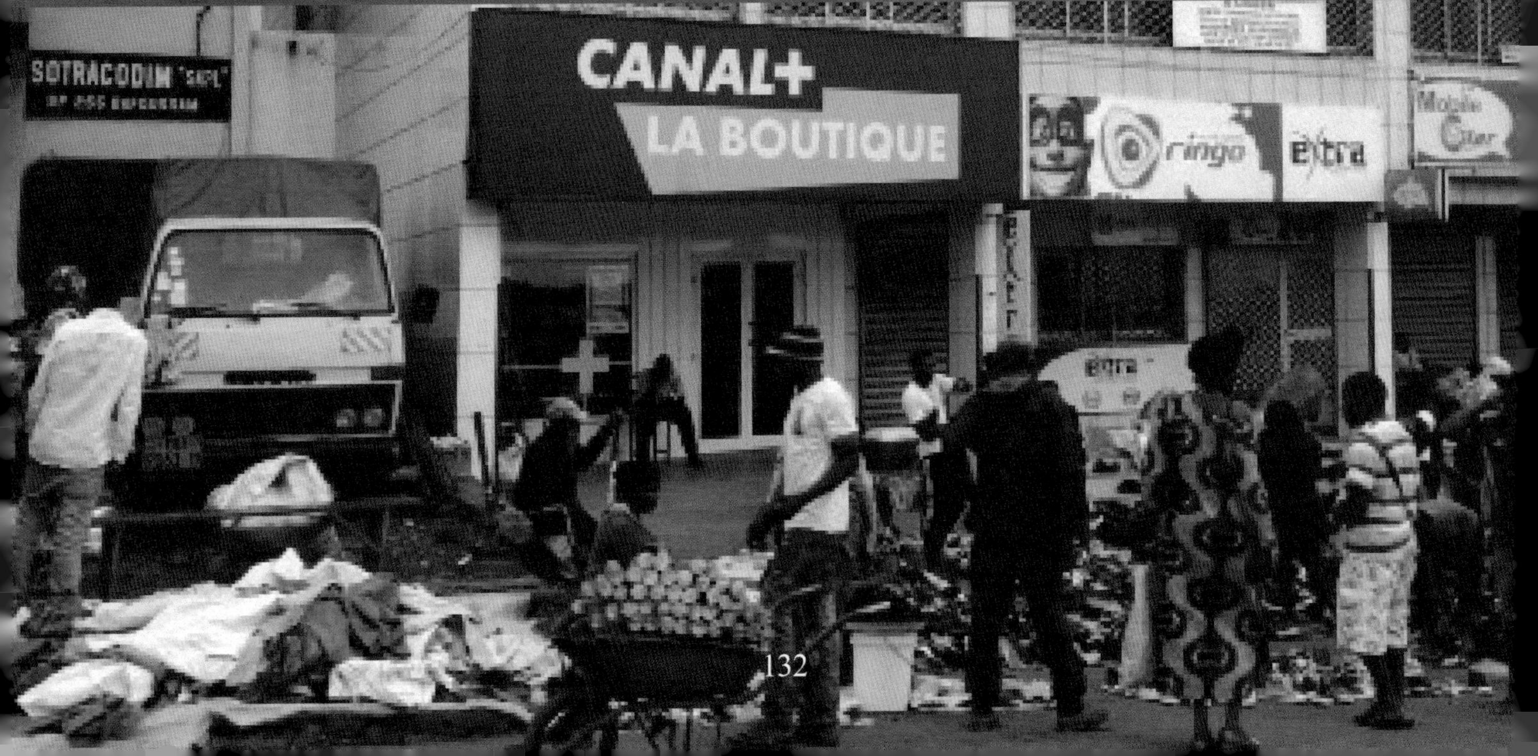

A DAY TRIP TO BAMENDA
DAY 9

After a breakfast of "real" Cameroonian coffee (not instant NesCafé) and rolls, we took a day trip to Bamenda in West Cameroon, an English-speaking former British protectorate. On the previous day we had arranged to hire a driver from the hotel for the day. The owner of Et Feh Technology Garage, our driver, picked us up in an older car. It was well-used, and as the day went on we realized that it needed new shocks. We began our trip on a day with crisp air and lots of fluffy white clouds. The scenery was magnificent. It rained on and off during the whole day, but not enough to ruin our trip. After filling up the gas tank at a local gas station, we took the mountain road to Bamenda. This busy highway snakes through the hills

A typical farm on the road to Bamenda

A street scene on the way to Bamenda

and mountains, crosses numerous rivers and streams, and connects towns and villages where farmers sell and ship their produce.

Well-tended farms could be seen all along the way. The terraced gardens along the side of the hills were especially beautiful. We frequently came across areas where all sorts of agricultural products were being loaded on trucks.

Since it was Sunday, there were a lot of people walking on the side of the road. They were dressed in their best clothes, going and coming from church. Another frequent sight was the crowds at the local outdoor markets, which were mostly held in the center of the towns and villages.

A trip that should take about 90 minutes dragged on for about two and a half hours – all because of the deteriorating road. Of all of the main highways I've traveled on, this one was definitely the worst. Our driver told us that the road was in the process of being repaved. We saw evidence of some work on bridges and the areas around Bamenda, but nothing concerning the pot holes. Pot holes and ruts were not the only obstacles; there were the speed bumps that seemed to appear out of nowhere causing the driver to brake

A Sunday gathering in a tov on the way to Bamenda

SUNDAY MARKET SCENES

These photos were taken of several Sunday markets in towns and villages along the road to Bamenda.

Bamenda from above

hard. Our driver generally drove too fast and for some reason continually maneuvered over the speed bumps on an angle to lessen the jolt. Then there were the toll stations and car inspection road blocks to check truck weight, driver's licenses, and seatbelt use. The system seemed to be working. Despite the terrible road, we didn't see a single accident.

Bamenda is situated in a valley at the base of a high cliff. Coming into town, you see the whole city come into view, and what a spectacular view it is! The city is considerably larger than I remembered it. Then, it reminded me of a town with a small central area with bad roads. Today, it is a sprawling city with paved roads and tall buildings. It has a "British flavor;" that is hard to find today. The single most visible building is the Blue Mosque in the center of town.

During our short time in Bamenda, I noticed that people spoke both English and French, unlike in the eastern and southern parts of the country where French is the primary language and little English is spoken, Although English is taught as the primary language in schools in West Cameroon, Pidgin English is widely spoken on the street. While doing research on the Internet, I've read reports of unrest with political overtones among the English-speaking population, due to the lack of representation at the federal government

A view of the main street from the balcony of the Dreamland Restaurant

level. The basic fear seems to be that the partnership that was promised when West and East Cameroon became united has turned out to be its total assimilation into the culture of the dominating French-speaking sphere. To counter this, there is even discussion about seceding and becoming its own country. As a stamp collector, I've even come across a design of stamps for an independent Southern Cameroon.

It was raining on and off when we got to the center of town. We looked for a restaurant for lunch and ended up at the Dreamland Restaurant. It's a large restaurant with a bar, eating area, and an entertainment area. We were the only ones in the restaurant. By the time we left there only two other groups of people eating. We had the grilled chicken and French fries with our usual beer.

Afterwards, we took a quick tour of the city. We went to the artisan center and a bookstore, but they were closed because it was Sunday. Before heading back to Bafoussam, we visited the Blue Mosque, which was located on a narrow street. We walked around for a few minutes, looked inside, and left. We were careful not to enter the mosque because we didn't know if Darleen, being a woman, would be allowed in. I wasn't looking forward to our trip back to Bafoussam, knowing that we would have to take the same road back.

On our two and a half hour drive back it rained most of the time, and I found myself nodding off at times only to be awakened by sudden braking to avoid the potholes, ruts, and speed bumps. When we got to the hotel, we went directly to the bar where we had a "real" drink: vodka with orange juice – my first during the trip! It was great, but very expensive. We didn't eat dinner that night. We only had peanuts, provided by the bar, and a bag of trail mix that I had brought with me. I got to sleep about 9 p.m. after writing in my notebook.

New construction

The main mosque

138

English language signs

A DAY TRIP TO FOUMBAN
DAY 10

The sultan's palace

I got up early. While getting ready, I watched TV and got caught up on the news, especially the news from the shopping mall takeover by terrorists in Nairobi, Kenya.

I met Darleen for breakfast and planned our day trip to Foumban, about an hour's drive away. The road was in much better condition than the one to Bamenda. We had the same crazy driver who drove too fast, passed on curves, and didn't talk at all. We stopped to buy gas and began our day trip.

Our first stop was at the Sultan's Palace. The building was built in the early 1900s and has been renovated since our last visit. The court yard was full of men scurrying around doing their business. We paid for admission to the palace and were given a tour by a little old man. There was only one other tourist: a young Frenchman, who was disappointed not being able to take photos. The tour lasted about an hour and was extensive. The lighting was poor and the floor creaked. The museum objects were very interesting and it was evident that they had been there for a long time. Hopefully, with the construction of a newly planned museum, they will be displayed better.

Next, we went to an attractive nearby restaurant named Chez Tata Mimi for lunch. There was only one other person eating there. There wasn't much of a choice;

The sultan's palace in 1971

Darleen in Foumban in 1971

THE SULTAN'S PALACE

WILLKOMMEN

RESTAURANT
CHEZ TATA MIMI
PETIT DEJEUNER
TOUS METS AFRICAINS
ET OCCIDENTAUX
SERVICE TRAITEUR
LOCATION CHAISES
COUVERTS
MARMITES CHAUFFANTES
OUVERT 7ʲ/7
LA BRAISE
TOUS LES SOIRS
TEL. 97 81 88 53

Men sitting in front of portraits of former sultans in the courtyard in front of the Sultan's palace

A wall mural in the courtyard

142

A model of the future museum

so we had chunks of beef in a red sauce on a bed of rice. Darleen and I looked at each other as if to ask "Should we eat this?" We were afraid of the sauce, but we ate it anyway because we were really hungry. It was among one of the most delicious meals I've had in Cameroon. Fortunately, we didn't have any bad reactions afterwards. Looking back, I wish I had had more of it.

After lunch we went to the artisan center. We had hoped to find some bargains, but we didn't. The shop keepers were relentless in their requests to visit their stalls. We visited a few stalls and came away with only a few brass bracelets and bamboo vases. It was a disappointing visit so we decided to go back to the artisan outdoor market in Yaoundé when we returned where there was more of a variety of handcrafted items.

Next, we went to the sprawling central outdoor market. The market is spread out over a large area covering several blocks. It was full of people and it contained everything: vegetables, fruit, cooked food, palm oil, live chickens in baskets, butcher shops, shoe shops, clothing and tailor shops, and you-name-it. I bought some hot peppers with the idea of drying their seeds and bringing them back home so that I could plant them next spring. I wanted to make some of the Cameroon style hot pepper sauce that I grew fond of. We looked for Cameroonian designed cloth. Most of the cloth was imported from Nigeria. We found only one design that we liked. We would have bought more, but the price was too high. Again, we decided to wait to buy more cloth when we got back to Yaoundé.

143

Finally, we headed back to Bafoussam. Before returning to our hotel, we stopped to change more money, visited an outdoor bookstore where I bought two books on the history of Cameroon, and went shopping at a supermarket for food. Since we knew that we would have a kitchen at our hotel in Kribi, we decided to buy some staples: bread, salt, condensed milk, coffee, olive oil, a few spices, jam, water, sodas, cheese, tuna fish, cookies, and a few other items.

We finally arrived at the hotel and did very little for the rest of the evening. We checked our emails in the lobby, confirmed our reservations for a driver for our trip to Kribi, and went to the bar for peanuts and a screwdriver. Again, we were the only people in the restaurant and bar so we relaxed with our drinks and watched CNN before going to bed.

Seamstresses in the outdoor market

FOUMBAN'S OUTDOOR MARKET

DRIVING TO KRIBI
DAY 11

After our usual breakfast, we checked out of the hotel. We didn't have enough cash to pay for the hotel so I used my credit card. Darleen paid dollars for the cost of the driver. The exchange rate was not very favorable and the loss was considerable.

We had the same driver on our trip to Kribi. However, the car was different and fairly new and had air conditioning. The trip took most of the day: seven and half hours. We had filled the previous car's gas tank and didn't want to have to pay full price to fill this car's tank, too. The hotel arranged to give the driver money for gas.

Leaving Bafoussam heading toward Douala, we went through breathtaking mountain scenery. The road is a major route. It is very busy and is used by many trucks. The worse part of the trip had to do with our driver, who kept us on the edge of our seats with his fast and erratic driving. At one point it got to be too much for me to take so I complained about passing cars on curves. It didn't seem to make any difference; he kept on driving fast and taking chances.

At one point the driver slowed down when there were clumps of tall grass in the middle of the road. Instead of orange emergency cones, clumps of grass are used to signal drivers that there is an accident.

We finally came across a major accident that involved a large truck, a bus, and a motorcycle. The bus and truck were overturned at the side of the road and the motorcycle was crushed. The truck had been carrying hundreds of empty beer crates that ended up all over the road. By the time we arrived at the scene, people were already cleaning up the mess. We did not see any injured people if there had been any because they would have been moved earlier. Seeing the accident didn't seem to bother the driver because he kept on driving too fast. As we neared Douala, we asked our driver to stop to rest and have a short picnic with the food that we had brought. He said no and kept on driving. We didn't eat anything until we reached Kribi seven and a half hours later.

Douala was a driving nightmare. Hundreds of trucks, cars, and motorcycles jammed the road leading to the

146

Above the clouds on our way from Bafoussam to Douala

Worri Bridge which connects the western part of the country to Douala. There was a perpetual traffic jam getting through Douala. The worst road I've ever seen was between the Worri Bridge and downtown Douala. The road was wide and the pavement had been badly worn and used. Instead of pot holes, there were craters that reduced the flow of traffic to a crawl. Instead of staying on one's own side of the road, there was a free for all. Drivers took advantage of any opening to get through this confusion of organized chaos. To make matters worse, pedestrians kept dodging traffic crossing the street. Luckily, we didn't witness any accidents. We could see the high-rise buildings of downtown Douala from a distance, but didn't go there. We kept to the outskirts of the city, looking for the highway to Edea. Unfamiliar with the area, our driver took a secondary road to Edea by mistake. It was a one lane unpaved road through thick jungle. From the number of cars that we encountered on this road, it was evident that this was an isolated area. We drove by small villages and individual houses. There were no stores, gas stations, or any other businesses. However, we did see a few village schools and churches. Again, our driver was in a hurry and drove too fast. While rounding a curve in the road at high speed, we came upon a large ditch that couldn't be avoided. Our driver couldn't stop in time and drove right into the ditch. The car stopped suddenly and I hit my head on the ceiling of the car. We all survived without any injuries. We continued for a short distance before discovering that the car had a flat tire. We stopped by the roadside and the driver changed the tire. Luckily there was a spare. Had there not been a spare, we would have had to wait a long time because we were in a remote area with very little traffic. This was the first time during our whole trip that we got out of the car. By this time, Darleen and I were not on speaking terms with the driver. All we wanted was to get to Kribi as fast as possible.

View of the Worri River and downtown Douala in the distance.

Unlike the dense forest of the southern part of the country, the landscape on the road from Bafoussam to Douala is hilly and covered with many farms.

Despite our issues with the driver, the scenery along this out-of-the-way road was beautiful, just like one would expect to see in an old Tarzan movie.

After an hour and a half on this road, we arrived in Edea. We crossed the Sanaga Bridge and saw the large hydro-electric plant and the large aluminum plant nearby.

Senaga River water fall at Ed

148   *Flat tire on the way to Edea from Douala*

Palm oil plantations between Edea and Kribi

Welcome to Douala

We breathed a sigh of relief when we found the main road to Kribi. The road is flat, straight, and well-maintained. Along the sides of the road were large expanses of numerous palm oil plantations, which employ many of the locals and are run by a Swiss company. The road continued along the coast, providing beautiful views of white sandy beaches, jagged black rock formations, and swaying palm trees.

At last we arrived in Kribi, which turned out to be a little piece of paradise. Although Kribi is a city, it has the feel of a town. The center of town is located around the port area and is made up of a commercial center, an outdoor food market, a large fish market, a marina, and a few resort hotels that cater to foreign tourists and well-to-do Cameroonians from other parts of the country. It is a popular destination, especially during the dry season, when the ocean breezes provide relief from the heat. We happened to arrive during the rainy season, which coincides with the beginning of the school year and the tourist off-season. During our stay, the atmosphere was quiet and relaxed. (Before our trip we tried to make reservations at some of the other hotels, but they were all closed for the season.)

Our hotel, Les Gites de Kribi, was fantastic. It is located a few miles south of Kribi along the main road to the Lobé Falls. We were fortunate to come here even though we were the only guests at the resort. I'm glad that we kept our visit to Kribi for the last part of our trip. After a long wait we could finally wind down from the whirlwind of traveling throughout the country.

Douala street scene

LES GÎTES DE KRIBI HOTEL

Our bungalow

The bedrooms can sleep up to six.

The living room had a TV and air conditioning

The kitchen had everything we needed.

The view from our bungalow

Instead of hotel rooms, we stayed in a bungalow with a living room with air conditioning and a flat-screen TV, two bedrooms, two bathrooms with hot water, and a kitchen with a microwave, hot plate, refrigerator and cooking utensils. It even had an outdoor patio with a picnic table.

The hotel also had a large swimming pool, jacuzzi, exercise room, library, and outside cooking grills. Surprisingly, Wi-Fi was also available in our bungalow, but only for the first day. When it stopped working, we had to use the community room to check our emails. It seemed that Mr. Decieux, the owner of the hotel, was the only one who could reset the Wi-Fi; nobody else knew how to fix it. Unfortunately, Mr. Decieux was away on business in France and was expected back the day we were scheduled to leave. Mr. Decieux is a former French ship captain who married a Cameroonian, Janette. After his retirement, they settled in Kribi and recently opened a resort and restaurant.

The library   *The pool and hot tub*

LE PLAISIR DU GOUT RESTAURANT

The best part of our stay in Kribi was the Le Plaisir du Gout Restaurant and Bar, which was located just across the street from our hotel. It is by far the best (and only) restaurant and bar in town. It is positioned on the ocean's edge only a few feet from the water. At high tide, the waves hit the base of the structure to the point that sandbags are needed to prevent erosion of the foundation. The restaurant has a nautical feel and is decorated with dark wood walls and furniture, model ships, and other maritime inspired decorations. Another impressive part of the restaurant was its kitchen, which was large, clean and openly visible to the diners.

One unexpected sight was a large collection of Cameroonian postage stamps displayed under thick glass on the bar tables overlooking the ocean. The stamps were part of Mr. Decieux's collection. I went to Cameroon in hope of finding someone who collected stamps so that I could trade or buy some. I basically gave up, except for visiting the philatelic office in Yaoundé. Then, I saw the stamps displayed in the bar. There were several envelopes with old stamps that were of considerable value. I desperately wanted to talk to Mr. Decieux about his collection, but he was in France.

After settling in, we went to the restaurant, had a cocktail and freshly roasted peanuts on the patio and watched one of the most spectacular sunsets I've ever seen. This was truly paradise! We decided to have dinner on the restaurant patio. Darleen had fish and I had chicken in peanut sauce, a dish that I had been looking forward to. It was delicious! We went back to the hotel, and I went to bed after writing about the day's events in my notebook.

EXPLORING KRIBI
DAY 12

On our second day in Kribi, we made our own breakfast: coffee, bread, butter, and jam. We ate at the picnic table just outside our bungalow door. We had a beautiful view of the ocean, but we had to eat fast because of ants. We also had to be careful inside, too. Ants could be found anywhere there was food, especially on the kitchen table. Before using the table, we had to wipe it down and spray bug repellent on the floor and at the base of the legs of the table.

We decided to take a walk along the beach on our way to the center of town, where we planned to buy fish

A child and a woman on the beach washing clothes in a fresh water stream that flows into the ocean

and vegetables for our evening meal. Being in a resort town where the locals were used to foreigners, I decided to wear shorts, a T-shirt, and tennis shoes. We walked along a beautiful and mostly deserted beach. We saw only a few people along the way. The waves were small so we took off our shoes and walked along the edge of the water. When

The marina, restaurant, and bar

we got to Kribi, our first site was a small marina with only a few pleasure boats. We stopped at the marina restaurant and bar and had a beer and peanuts. The marina restaurant provides a wonderful view of the port, the Catholic cathedral, and the newly built fish market, which was built with a grant from the Japanese government.

The Catholic church and the fish market

A view of the fish market from the bridge

We made our way to the fish market which was only a few steps away. The market contains scores of stalls where local fishermen sell their catches. As fishermen arrived, the fish were brought to concrete slabs and sold to the highest bidders. We bought two lobsters and a few pounds of large shrimp. Then, we searched for an outside vegetable market. We found the market tucked away behind some stores in the center of town. It was a traditional market with narrow, rutted, and uneven paths along rows of stalls. We bought tomatoes, onions, parsley, and garlic. On our way back to our hotel we stopped by a supermarket where we bought bread, some cheese, and yogurt. Carrying the ingredients for our dinner, we walked back to the hotel along the main road. It was hot, humid and threatening to rain. The walk seemed to take forever, and I was totally exhausted by the time we got back to the hotel. Before taking a short nap, I spoke to one of the hotel

Seafood is sold on tiled slabs throughout the market

Shopping for fish in 197

Shopping for fish at the same place today

Yum, yum! Grilled seafood!

Nice shirt.

Our dinner

Another day in paradise!

employees about using the outside grill. The employee was the night watchman, who was in his 60s. He was very friendly and went out of his way to help us. He said that he would clean it, find some charcoal, and have someone start the grill later that evening.

During sunset and after our evening beer and peanuts on the patio of the restaurant, we went back to our bungalow to clean the lobsters and shrimps. About the same time, a young man appeared and said that he would start the grill. We grilled the lobster tails and the largest shrimps, leaving the smaller shrimps for the next day's meal. To accompany the main dish, we made a small salad. The lobsters and shrimps were sweet and delicious; it was a very satisfying meal. We then watched a little television, checked our emails, and went to bed.

Cheers!

LOBÉ RIVER & FALLS
DAY 13

The Lobe River

On our last full day in Kribi we decided to visit Lobé Falls, located about ten miles south of Kribi. The waterfalls are among the few in the world that drop directly into the ocean. We arranged with the hotel to hire a driver for the day. Our driver's name was Edie Patric Mimvouna. He was young, bright, and very intelligent. And, he drove carefully and responsibly. He was friendly and a good conversationalist. We learned a lot about life in Kribi and about living in Cameroon in general from him.

First we went to the Lobé River where we met one of our driver's friends. He arranged for us to take an hour-long canoe trip along the river. Our

Our guide

guide paddled us upstream and stopped midway to take a walk through the jungle. Remembering our visit to the Mefou Primate Sanctuary, I was a little nervous because I was wearing shorts and light shoes with no socks. Fortunately it was a short walk along a path that was hardly visible. Happily, we didn't encounter any ants. Our guide concentrated on explaining the medicinal uses of the many plants we encountered. On the way back we went with the flow of the river. The ride was so quiet that we could hear the sounds of the jungle. Our guide offered to take us to a Pigmy village further up the river, but we decided not to go. Pigmies are an oddity and

162

THE LOBE RIVER

discriminated against in Cameroon. We didn't want to see more poverty or gawk at them. The only other people we saw were Chinese in another canoe. We waved to each other and went on our separate ways. They were probably from the new port that is being built by the Chinese government about twelve miles south of the river.

When we got back to the shore at the base of the bridge over the Lobé River, our driver took us to Lobé Falls only a few minutes away. The Lobé Falls extend for about a thousand yards in a shallow bay surrounded by a long white sandy beach. Again, we took another canoe ride. This time it was to see the falls close up. We took off our shoes and waded into the water to get into the canoe. We were taken through a small bay and went within a few feet of the falls. It was an exhilarating experience being so close and feeling the spray from the falls. When we returned to where we started, we visited a few souvenir shops and passed by

163

A walk through the jungle

Along the river bank

an outdoor restaurant where a few Chinese men were having lunch, eating shrimp, and drinking beer.

When we got back to our hotel, we went directly to our usual place on the patio of the restaurant and had our usual beer and peanuts while watching another spectacular sunset. Then, we went back to our bungalow and prepared dinner. We cooked the peeled shrimp that we had cleaned the day earlier with some crushed tomatoes and piment in olive oil and butter along with a little curry powder. We served this over a bed of rice. We had water with our meal. We finished our meal with a few butter cookies and a chocolate bar. Before going to bed, we checked our emails and watched a little television.

Chinese workers on an outing

The beach near the falls

THEN & NOW

The falls and me in 1970 (above) and in 2013 (below)

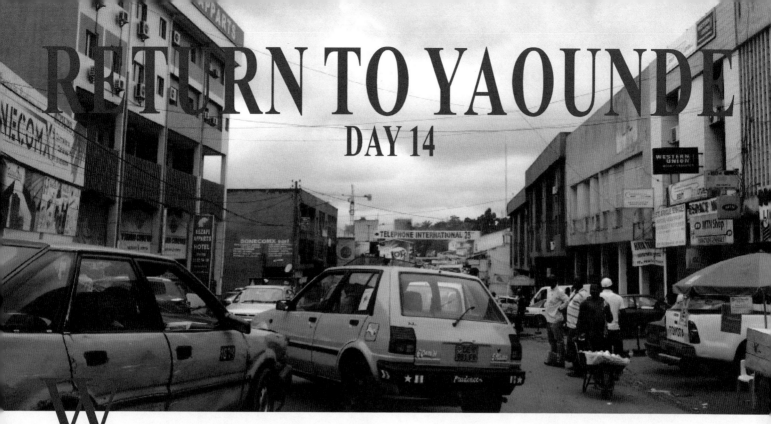

RETURN TO YAOUNDE
DAY 14

We were lucky to meet Mr. Decuieu and his wife just as we were leaving. They invited us to their home where we spent about half an hour. What a house! It was just like something we would see in France: large living room/dining room, big flat screen TV and all the trappings of luxury. Our driver was anxious to leave so we had to cut our visit short. It would have been wonderful to have spent more time with them.

I really didn't want to leave Kribi. Our stay there was not long enough. I could have stayed there for a few more weeks. Although our stopover was only a few days long, our visit to Kribi was by far the best experience I've ever had in Cameroon. If I ever go back to Cameroon, Kribi would be the first and only place in the country I would go to.

Our trip to Yaoundé took about four hours and was very pleasant. The road was good, the terrain flat, and the scenery beautiful. The highway is a major artery between the country's two largest cities: Douala and Yaoundé.

We passed through many towns and villages. Even though there was a lot of truck traffic, toll stops, and commuter traffic entering Yaoundé, the trip seemed fast.

We went directly to our hotel where we checked into the same rooms we had had at the beginning of our trip.

We rested and took a nap. Then, we went up to the rooftop restaurant to have dinner. What we found was the preparation for a wedding. We were told that we would have to eat in the downstairs restaurant that evening. However, we were allowed to have a beer on the rooftop patio before the wedding reception started. It started to rain heavily, so we went inside and watched television and observed the employees scurrying around taking care of last minute details for the wedding reception.

Eventually, we went to the lobby to check our emails and had dinner. We had the usual, grilled zebu steak and French fries. Then, I went to my room, watched television, and wrote in my notebook before going to bed.

Mr. & Mrs. Decuieu

167

OUR LAST DAY
DAY 15

We got up and had breakfast around 9 o'clock. We had to find something to do for the entire day because our flight to Paris wasn't scheduled to leave until 11 o'clock at night. We checked out of our hotel and left our baggage in the hotel storage room behind the reception desk. We called our former driver, Dieu-Donné, and hired him for the day. This was the day to take care of loose ends.

It was nice to see Dieu-Donné again. We felt comfortable with him. First we changed money at the same place we did on our first day. Next, we went back to the artisan center where I bought more snake skin wallets and Darleen bought a batik table cloth. Then, Dieu-Donné called one of his friends about buying official Cameroon soccer team jerseys. He drove us to the back of a small hotel in the center of town where we met a man who had a bag of shirts. Apparently, the jerseys are hard to get and cost a lot. At first the vendor wanted the equivalent of $50 per shirt. We eventually bought four for $20 apiece. Next, Dieu-Donné took us to a nearby store that specialized in cloth. We found five different patterns and paid about $10 per bolt. (When I got home, I had two tablecloths made from one of the bolts.) I also bought a handmade dress shirt as a present for my spouse.

By this time, it was lunch and we went back to the Café de Yaoundé where we had a long, long, lunch. Before leaving the restaurant we sat in the lush garden and had a free glass of a liqueur that the owner gave us.

Finally, we took a drive through the Bastos neighborhood and stopped at a coffee house where we experienced the environment of the "upper class" Cameroonians and expatriates. It's a comfortable place similar to those one would find in any other big city around the world.

We went back to our hotel in the late afternoon where we spent time on the rooftop restaurant and bar. We also spent a lot of time waiting in the lobby where we checked our emails and just hung out. During the whole time we were in the lobby, there was a man sitting next to us using his laptop computer. He eventually introduced himself to us. He is a Christian evangelical pastor who wanted to talk about his church. We just listened until we were rescued by Dieu-Donné who was scheduled to take us to the airport.

The airport is a mad house. There is so much activity that it was hard to concentrate on keeping our luggage safe and in sight at all times. Dieu-Donné got a porter to take our baggage and we followed them to the Air France check-in area. We paid Dieu-Donné for the day, gave him a generous tip, and gave him our telephone because we no longer had any need for it. We finally said good-bye, and we were on our own. By this time

Aa coffee house in the Bastos section of Yaounde

we had used all of our Cameroonian money except for the bills I wanted to take home as souvenirs and 10,000 francs that we would need to pay the exit fee.

Check in took time and went smoothly. We had to go through three different security checkpoints before we boarded the plane. The last check was done by Air France employees because, as I was told, the airline didn't trust the government's security checks.

We boarded the plane, had a quick meal and slept for most of the flight back to Paris.

When we got to Paris, Darleen and I split up. She stayed in France to stay with friends and visit other parts of Europe for another month. I went to another terminal to wait for my flight to Los Angeles. I had three hours to spend so I went shopping for cheese and foie gras with the extra euros I had. I took a little nap in a large slumber chair and almost missed my flight. I had forgotten that there was one hour difference between French and Cameroon time so I had to run to make the flight on time. Once on board, I was annoyed that I had the same uncomfortable seat that I had coming to France. I paid extra for the seat which was next to an exit and had no seat in front of it. The seat was so narrow that I couldn't fit into it comfortably. I complained and was given another seat at the back of the plane. During the whole trip, I became more and more sick. I had to use the rest room every hour due to severe diarrhea, which, I believe, was due to the meal I had on the flight from Cameroon to France. I was also very dehydrated and couldn't drink enough water.

Passing through passport and customs was dreadful because I felt so bad. My husband, Michael, met me at the airport with our dog, Bella, and took me to a convenience store on the way home to buy a large bottle of Gatorade that I drank in one gulp. I went directly to bed when I got home.

Because of our thorough planning and a large dose of serendipity, our flexibility, and a superb travel partner, my trip was totally successful and extremely satisfying. After a few months of editing photos

A 1983 Cameroonian stamp celebrating human rights

and my daily logs, this e-book is the result. I hope I provided some general information as well as some insights into Cameroonian life that may be useful for travelers who plan on visiting Cameroon.

As a final note, I know that I will probably never visit Cameroon again. It's not that I wouldn't want to, but the thought of not feeling welcomed as a gay person is not a challenge I want to undertake especially at this stage of my life.

Some day I hope that all Cameroonian authorities will finally recognize human rights for all -- including mine.

De Gaulle's Air France terminal

LAST WORDS

from Darleen's Travel Log

This expedition was hard—so many mixed emotions, frequent meltdowns in the hotel room at night after witnessing such abject poverty, the scrambling to get money out of us that was wearing me down. We felt "street smart" enough from having traveled to so many other countries, but this was difficult. There was no infrastructure for tourism and I had the impression that we had to invent things as we went along. Being the only "white" tourists in what seemed like the whole country made it especially arduous.

Made in the USA
Charleston, SC
10 February 2017